US SAILING

Basic Keelboat

The national standard for quality sailing instruction

Published by the UNITED STATES SAILING ASSOCIATION Copyright © 2014 by the UNITED STATES SAILING ASSOCIATION.
All rights reserved. No part of this publication may be reproduced, stored in a retrieval system, or transmitted, in any form or by
any means, electronic, mechanical, photocopying, recording, or otherwise without prior written permission from the
UNITED STATES SAILING ASSOCIATION.
ISBN 9781-938915-06-2
Printed in the United States of America.
UNITED STATES SAILING ASSOCIATION P.O. Box 1260, 15 Maritime Drive, Portsmouth, RI 02871-0907
www.ussailing.org
www.sailingcertification.com

Cover Image: A Colgate 26, courtesy of Offshore Sailing School

Acknowledgments

The US Sailing Keelboat Certification System and this book are the result of many people working together as a team. But without the initial and ongoing support of Robert H. Hobbs, James P. Muldoon, John Bonds, the Board of Directors of US Sailing, the Commercial Sailing Committee, the Training Committee and Sail America, this program would not have been launched. In addition, representatives from various sailing schools, charter companies and the boating industry have shared their invaluable input and advice. Assisting the creative team for this book has been a privilege and an adventure for Tim Broderick and Timmy Larr who have put in many long hours. We would also like to thank John Rousmaniere, author of The Annapolis Book of Seamanship, who along with Designer/Editor Mark Smith originally developed a number of presentation concepts adapted for use in this book.

This edition of Basic Keelboat was significantly updated and improved thanks to the US Sailing National Faculty.

Mark Smith
Designer/Editor
A lifelong sailor, graphic designer, editor and illustrator, Mark is currently Creative Director for North Sails. Mark was editorial and art director for Yacht Racing/Cruising magazine (now Sailing World) from 1970-83, editor and publisher of Sailor magazine from 1984-86, and editor and art director of American Sailor from 1987-89. His works include design and illustration for the Annapolis Book of Seamanship, authored by John Rousmaniere and published by Simon and Schuster. Mark lives in Norwalk, CT with his wife Tina and daughters Stephanie, Natalie and Cristina.

Monk Henry
Writer
Several years ago Monk became involved with sailing on San Francisco Bay as he approached retirement from a career in television as director and producer. He is currently preparing for his next career as he fulfills his lifelong ambition to sail to parts unknown on his 36-foot ketch.

Kim Downing
Illustrator
Kim grew up sailing in the Midwest with his family. Sailing is a lifelong passion which he has now passed along to his wife and two sons. He is currently an Art Director for a major home improvement magazine, and also continues to provide technical illustration for numerous books and magazines within the marine industry. Recently Kim has achieved a personal goal as a US Sailing Level 1 Sailing Instructor, as well as helping to start a new sailing school for kids and adults within his local yacht club.

Rob Eckhardt
Illustrator
A graphic design professional, Rob was on the staff of SAIL Magazine and has many years of experience as a designer for advertising agencies, publications and his own business clients. He is a graduate of the Rochester Institute of Technology, Rochester, NY. Rob began sailing dinghies as a youngster and currently enjoys one-design racing and coastal cruising.

James Chen
Photographer
James' work has been featured in numerous publications and corporate marketing campaigns. He is the recipient of national and international photographic awards and is recognized for his archi-tectural photography. He has received an Honorary Master of Science in Professional Photography from the Brooks Institute of Photography. He enjoys occasional daysailing from his home in Santa Barbara, CA.

David Norton
Designer
An avid sailor who grew up racing dinghies on Naraganset Bay and cruising New England waters on his family's Pearson 36, Orion – David is currently the Associate Art Director for Cruising and Sailing World Magazines. David is an award-winning designer, and also Founder and Director of Harbor Creative, a creative services agency.

Foreword

Once you have spent time under sail, you will notice that people on sailboats tend to wave at each other. For many, sailing is a passion to be enjoyed for a lifetime. Ours is a sport that connects the generations and brings people together.

But sailing is challenging. And, in fact, at times can be dangerous. Therefore, safety at sea is of paramount importance.

To maximize your enjoyment on the water, you must have confidence in yourself, your boat, equipment and crew. *Basic Keelboat*, published by US Sailing, helps you learn to sail with all the skills required for safety at sea. For newcomers, careful study and practice is essential. When you're prepared, life under sail is more enjoyable.

For me, racing has been my primary focus. More recently, cruising, daysailing as well as racing boats of all sizes from Lasers to Maxis, have blended together in a rewarding lifestyle. The lessons learned in *Basic Keelboat* will provide a strong foundation to help you build your skills for the future.

Gary Jobson

CONTENTS

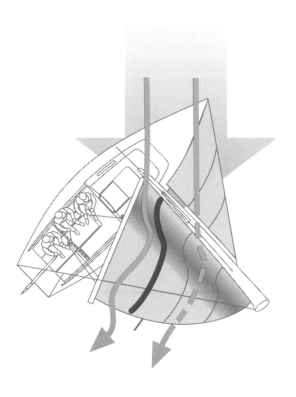

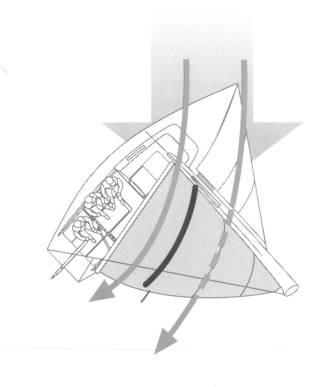

CONTENTS

Beam: Widest part of boat
Abeam?

✳

PARTS OF THE BOAT

Let's begin by learning some of the important parts on a boat and their names. Knowing some of these sailing terms will allow you to communicate better when on board the boat. Here's a quick overview.

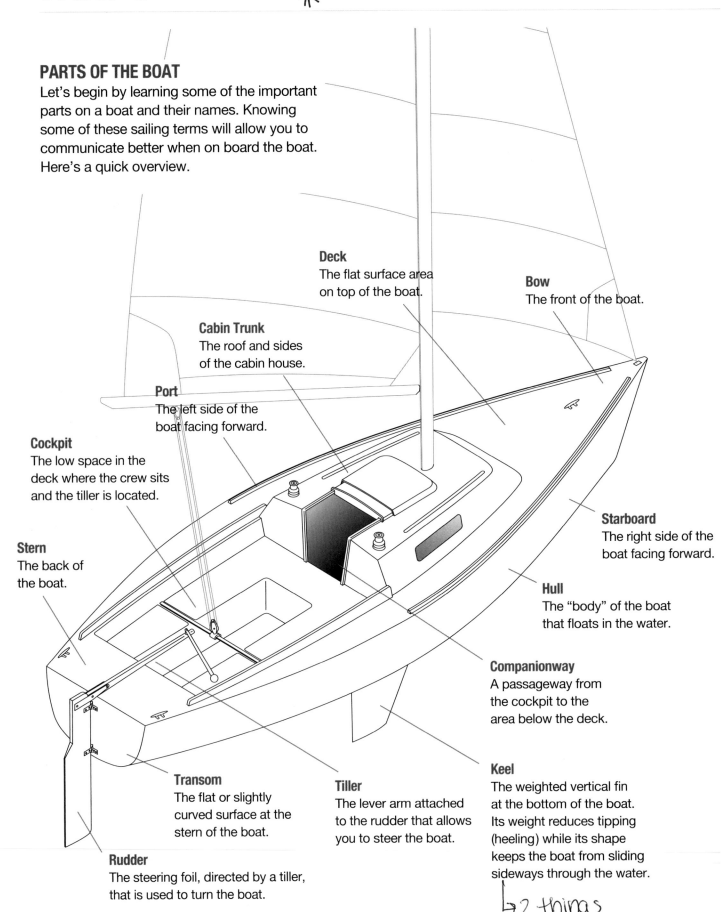

Deck
The flat surface area on top of the boat.

Bow
The front of the boat.

Cabin Trunk
The roof and sides of the cabin house.

Port
The left side of the boat facing forward.

Cockpit
The low space in the deck where the crew sits and the tiller is located.

Starboard
The right side of the boat facing forward.

Stern
The back of the boat.

Hull
The "body" of the boat that floats in the water.

Companionway
A passageway from the cockpit to the area below the deck.

Transom
The flat or slightly curved surface at the stern of the boat.

Tiller
The lever arm attached to the rudder that allows you to steer the boat.

Keel
The weighted vertical fin at the bottom of the boat. Its weight reduces tipping (heeling) while its shape keeps the boat from sliding sideways through the water.

Rudder
The steering foil, directed by a tiller, that is used to turn the boat.

2 things
1) Stability
2) prevent slide slipping

PARTS OF THE RIG

Now that you know your way around the deck, it's time to look up. The *rig* includes sails (*mainsail* and *jib*), spars (*mast* and *boom*), supporting wires (*standing rigging*) and sail controls (*running rigging*).

Forestay
The part of the rigging that is attached to the bow of the boat that keeps the mast from falling backward.

Jib
The forward sail that is attached to the forestay.

Spreader
Struts that extend from the side of the mast that keep it from bending sideways.

Telltales
Pieces of cloth, yarn, or tape that indicate wind flow over a sail.

Shrouds
Rigging wires extending up from the sides of the boat to the mast that keep the mast from falling to either side.

Boom
The horizontal spar extending back from the mast. The foot (*bottom*) of the mainsail is attached to it.

Mast
The vertical spar in the middle of the boat from which the sails are set.

Mainsail
The sail hoisted on the back side of the mast and attached to the boom.

Batten
A slat of fiberglass, plastic or wood inserted into a pocket in the sail to help it hold its shape.

Telltales
Pieces of cloth, yarn, or tape that indicate wind flow over a sail.

Backstay
The part of the rigging, attached from the top of the mast to the stern of the boat, that keeps the mast from falling forward.

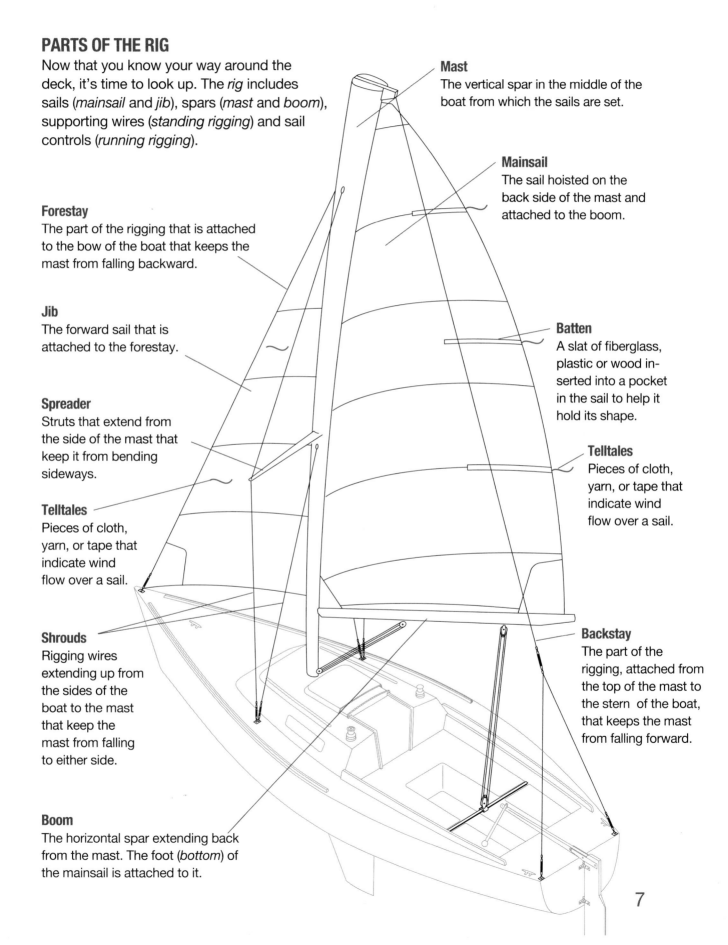

HOW A SAIL WORKS

Sails are a boat's engine, and they produce power in one of two ways. When the wind is coming from the side of the boat, it flows around both sides of the sail (like an airplane wing), creating lift which "pulls" the boat forward. When the wind is coming from behind the boat, it "pushes" against the sail and simply shoves the boat forward.

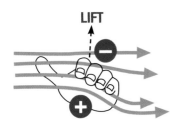

If you hold your hand out the window of a moving car, you can feel the force of the wind lifting your hand. This is the same force that "pulls" a sailboat forward when the wind comes over the side of the boat.

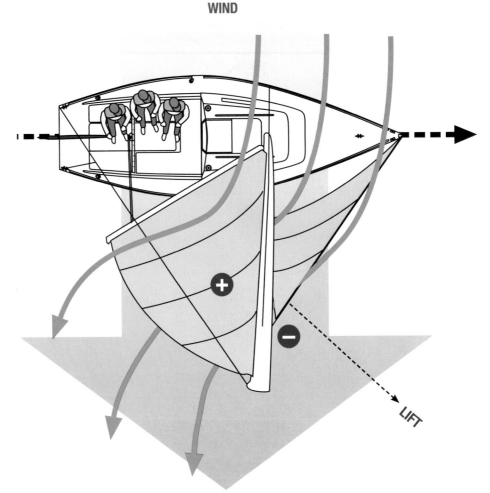

PULL MODE

Your sail is much more efficient at using the wind than your hand. It is shaped to bend the wind as it flows by, creating higher pressure on the inside of the sail ⊕ and lower pressure on the outside ⊖, thus creating lift. The lift the sail creates "pulls" the boat forward and sideways. The boat's keel keeps the boat from being pulled sideways through the water.

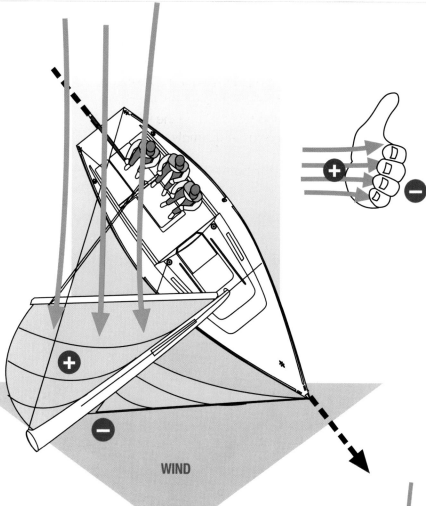

If you hold your hand out the window of a moving car with your palm facing the wind, you can feel the wind "push" your hand back. This is how a sail works when the wind is coming from behind.

WIND

PUSH MODE
With the wind coming from behind, the sail (and boat) are simply pushed forward through the water.

NO-GO
A sailboat cannot sail directly into the wind. You can try it, but your sails will only flap (luff) and you'll be dead in the water...or even start moving backward. Because there is no difference in wind pressure between one side of the sail and the other, the sail cannot generate either "push" or "pull." No push...no pull...NO GO!

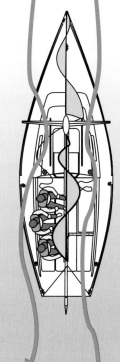

WIND

TRIMMING A SAIL

Many sailors view a boat's mainsheet and jib sheet as they would the accelerator on a car...the sails are sheeted (pulled) in until the sails stop luffing to make the boat go. As we described on the previous spread, a sail creates lift by redirecting wind flow. If the wind flows smoothly around (not past) the sails, maximum power is achieved, resulting in maximum boatspeed. If the sails are sheeted in or out too much, turbulent flow will result, reducing flow and slowing the boat.

Trimmed Just Right
▶ Smooth flow around sail
▶ Optimum power
▶ Optimum boat speed
▶ Easy steering
▶ Well-balanced

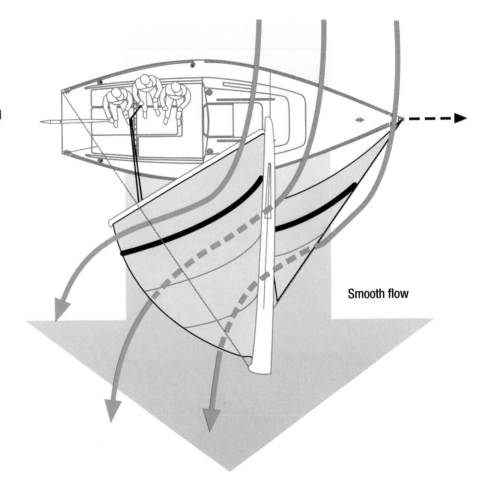

Smooth flow

Trimmed Too Loose

▶ Turbulent flow around sail
▶ Minimum power
▶ Reduced boat speed

Sailing with your sails trimmed too far out is not necessarily bad. There are times when you will want to sail along slowly (at less than maximum speed) and will trim in your sails only part way.

Sheet in sails to the point where they stop luffing to trim them correctly.

**Turbulent flow/
Minimum power**

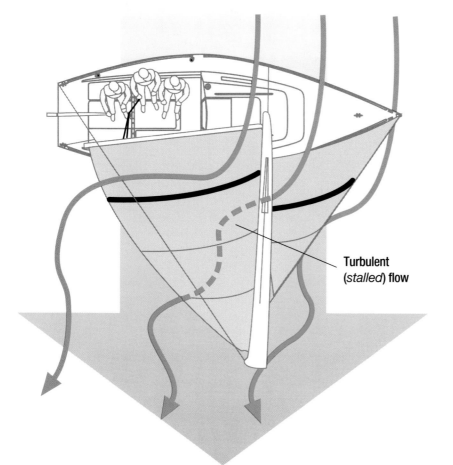

Trimmed Too Tight

▶ Turbulent flow around sail
▶ Reduced power
▶ Boat slows down
▶ Difficult steering
▶ Excessive heeling

If you lose wind flow around your sails, your boat will begin to feel sluggish. To get smooth flow going again, let out the sails until they luff, then bring them back in until they stop luffing and feel the boat pick up speed.

**Turbulent
(stalled) flow**

SAILING ACROSS THE WIND

Sailing across the wind, with the wind perpendicular to the side of the boat, is a fast and easy way to sail — certainly easier than sailing upwind. In your first lesson, you will spend a lot of time sailing across the wind, learning how to steer and trim the sails.

Reaching (sailing across the wind) is easy, fun, and lively. There's a slight heel to the boat, the sails are about half-way out, and it's easy to steer straight ahead or to the left or right.

These boats are sailing perpendicular to the wind with the wind coming over the side of the boat. This is called a beam reach.

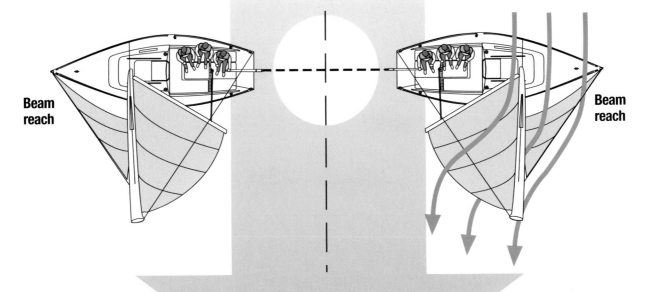

Beam
reach

Beam
reach

Checklist
▶ Feel the wind coming across the boat.
▶ Sheet the sails about halfway out.
▶ Steer toward an objective or landmark. Adjust the sails to changes in the boat's direction or changes in wind direction.

SAILING UPWIND

Although a boat cannot sail directly into the wind, it can sail upwind, or close to where the wind is coming from. Sailing about 45 degrees from the direction of the wind is about the closest a boat can sail upwind (although some high performance boats can sail as close as 30 to 35 degrees).

Sailing upwind is fun and exhilarating. You can feel waves passing under the hull, wind and spray in your face; knowing it is these natural elements that power the boat.

If you try to sail too close to the wind, your sails will luff and lose power, and the boat will come to a stop. This 90 degree area is called the No-Go Zone for obvious reasons.

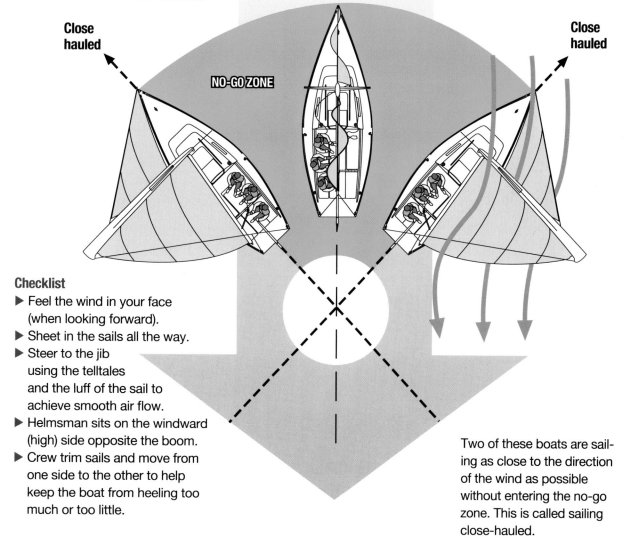

Close hauled

Close hauled

NO-GO ZONE

Checklist
▶ Feel the wind in your face (when looking forward).
▶ Sheet in the sails all the way.
▶ Steer to the jib using the telltales and the luff of the sail to achieve smooth air flow.
▶ Helmsman sits on the windward (high) side opposite the boom.
▶ Crew trim sails and move from one side to the other to help keep the boat from heeling too much or too little.

Two of these boats are sailing as close to the direction of the wind as possible without entering the no-go zone. This is called sailing close-hauled.

SAILING DOWNWIND

Sailing downwind, with the wind coming over the stern, is the most comfortable and relaxing point of sail. The wind and the waves are following you, the ride is smooth, and the boat stays upright. Sailing at a slight angle downwind (broad reach) is faster, safer, and easier than sailing directly downwind (with the wind coming directly behind the boat) because there is less chance for the boom to accidentally swing across the boat.

Sailing downwind is a very relaxing, "take it easy" way to sail with the wind at your back, your sails let out, and no spray.

Checklist
- ▶ Feel the wind on the back of your neck (when facing forward).
- ▶ Sheet out the sails so they're perpendicular to the wind.
- ▶ Adjust the sails to changes in boat or wind direction.
- ▶ Watch the jib as an early warning for an accidental jibe where the boom suddenly swings across the boat. If the jib goes limp and starts to cross the boat, head the boat toward the wind by pushing the tiller toward the boom until the jib returns and fills with wind again.

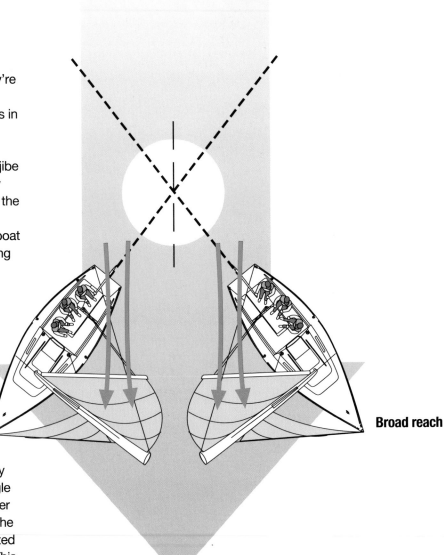

Broad reach

Broad reach

These boats are sailing away from the wind, but at an angle to it. The wind is blowing over the quarter (back corner of the boat) and the sails are sheeted perpendicular to the wind. This is called a broad reach.

POINTS OF SAIL

Close hauled (sailing upwind), **beam reach** (across the wind) and broad reach (downwind) are called *points of sail* by sailors.

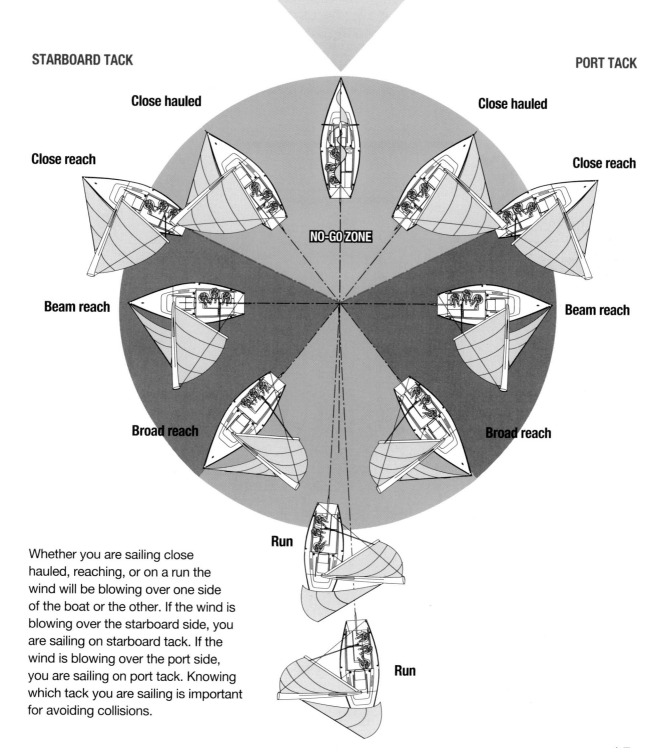

STARBOARD TACK

PORT TACK

Close hauled

Close hauled

Close reach

Close reach

NO-GO ZONE

Beam reach

Beam reach

Broad reach

Broad reach

Run

Run

Whether you are sailing close hauled, reaching, or on a run the wind will be blowing over one side of the boat or the other. If the wind is blowing over the starboard side, you are sailing on starboard tack. If the wind is blowing over the port side, you are sailing on port tack. Knowing which tack you are sailing is important for avoiding collisions.

HEADING UP AND BEARING AWAY

Whenever a boat turns to change direction, it is also turning relative to the wind—either heading up (toward) or bearing away (away) from the wind.

There are two key points to remember:
► To turn the boat, the tiller is pushed or pulled in the opposite direction that you want the boat to turn.
► Whenever a boat changes direction, both the mainsail and jib should be sheeted in or out accordingly.

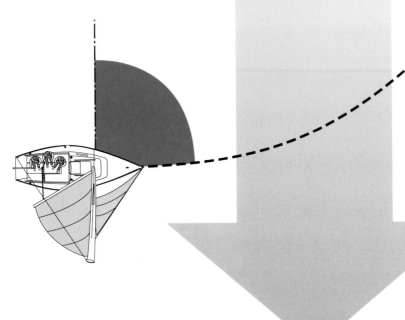

Angle to wind gets smaller

Heading Up
This boat is changing direction from sailing across the wind to sailing upwind by heading up.
► The helmsman pushes the tiller toward the boom.
► The crew trim in the sails all the way (close-hauled position).

Steering
► When a boat sails forward through the water, moving the tiller to port turns the boat to starboard.

► When a boat sails forward through the water, moving the tiller to starboard turns the boat to port.

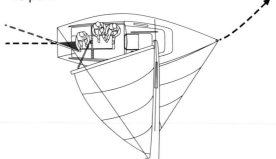

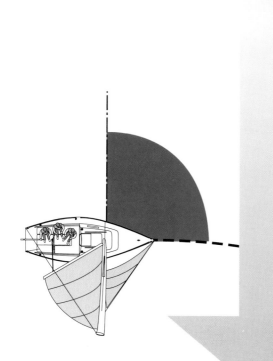

Bearing Away

This boat is changing direction from sailing across the wind to sailing downwind by bearing away.
- ▶ The helmsman pulls the tiller away from the boom.
- ▶ The crew ease out the sails almost all the way.

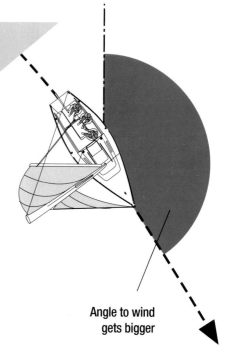

Angle to wind gets bigger

This boat has headed up into the No-Go Zone, and has not sheeted in the sails. The sails are flapping and have lost their power, so the boat will coast to a stop. Heading up into the No-Go Zone is often used to stop a boat, often in preparation of docking or picking up a mooring.

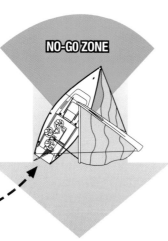

NO-GO ZONE

TACKING

A sailboat cannot sail directly into the wind. To make progress toward the wind it must sail a zig-zag course, much as you would use a series of angular switch-backs to reach the top of a steep hill. When a sailboat switches from a "zig" to a "zag," it is called a tack. A tack or tacking is turning the bow of a boat through the wind from one side of the No-Go Zone to the other. When a boat crosses the No-Go Zone, the sails will also cross the boat.

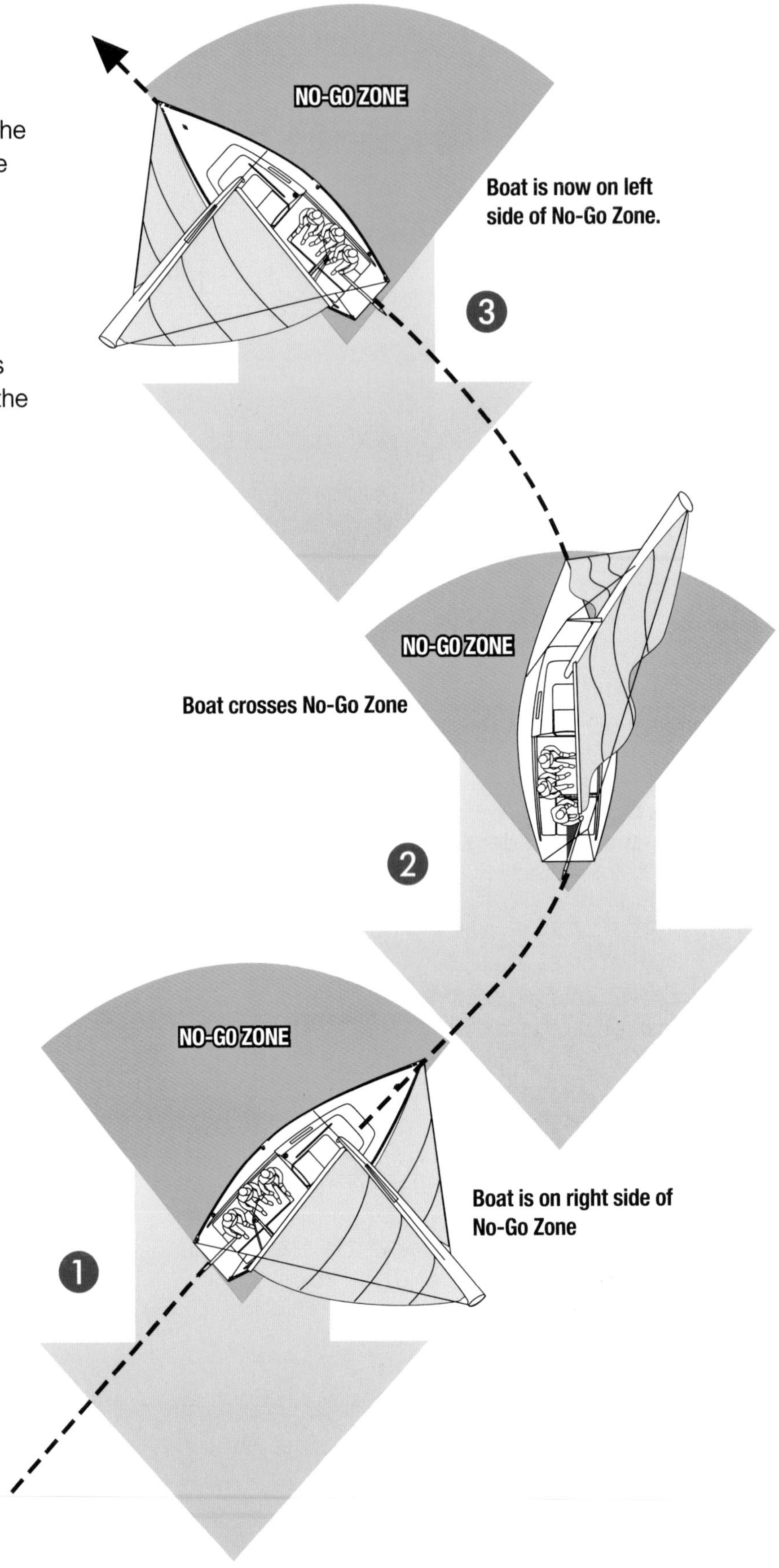

At the beginning of the tack ❶, the sailors are sailing close-hauled with the wind coming over the port side of the boat. In the middle of the tack ❷, the boat crosses the wind and No-Go Zone, and the sails lose all their power. In the final part of the tack ❸, their boat is again picking up speed, this time with the wind coming over starboard side of the boat. The boat's direction changed about 90 degrees.

NO-GO ZONE

Boat is now on left side of No-Go Zone.

❸

NO-GO ZONE

Boat crosses No-Go Zone

❷

NO-GO ZONE

Boat is on right side of No-Go Zone

❶

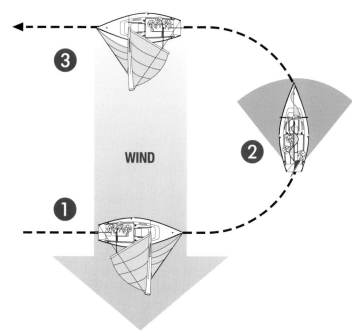

TACKING FROM REACH TO REACH

Tacking doesn't only happen when you are trying to sail toward the wind. Any time you switch the wind from one side of the boat to the other by sailing through the No-Go Zone, you are performing a tack. In the sequence to the left, the boat is reaching with the wind coming over the port side ❶, then sailing through the No-Go Zone ❷, and finally reaching with the wind coming over the starboard side ❸.

GETTING OUT OF IRONS

At some point while you are learning to sail, you will tack the boat too slowly through the wind and get stuck in the No-Go Zone. You are now in irons. The sails are luffing, the boat slows to a stop, and the rudder no longer steers the boat. It's a helpless feeling, but easily correctable.

Here's how:
❶ Sheet in one of the jib sheets (in this case the one on the port side) until the wind blowing over the bow makes the sail billow back toward you. This will push the boat backward and also push the bow off to one side. When the boat starts to move backward, move the tiller in the same direction as the bow is turning (in this case to the starboard side) to help the boat turn more quickly. When the wind is coming over the side of the boat ❷, release the jib sheet and trim it in on the other side. Then straighten the tiller, sheet in the mainsail, and off you go!

IN IRONS
The boat is pointed directly into the wind, both sails are luffing, the boat has come to a dead stop, and the rudder doesn't work since water has to be flowing past it to steer the boat.

WIND

JIBING

Another basic maneuver in sailing is the jibe. Like a tack, a jibe is a change in boat direction through the wind with the sails crossing from one side of the boat to the other. During a tack, you steer the bow through the wind (No-Go Zone). During a jibe, the wind crosses over the back of the stern.

At the beginning of the jibe ❶, the sails are let out almost all the way with the wind coming over the starboard side of the boat. In the middle of the jibe ❷, the stern of the boat crosses the wind and the sail swings over from one side to the other. A key to controlling the mainsail before it crosses over during a jibe is to sheet it in to the center of the boat before the stern crosses the wind. After the boom flops over, the mainsheet is let out quickly. Remember: *KEEP YOUR HEAD LOW AS THE BOOM SWINGS OVER!*
In the final part of the jibe ❸, the tiller is straightened and the mainsail is let back out almost all the way. The boat continues on with the wind coming over the port side of the boat.

NOTE: A "controlled" jibe helps minimize the speed of the boom crossing over. But in an uncontrolled jibe, the boom can whip across the cockpit quickly as the sail swings from one side to the other. An uncontrolled or *accidental jibe* (see opposite page) should be avoided.

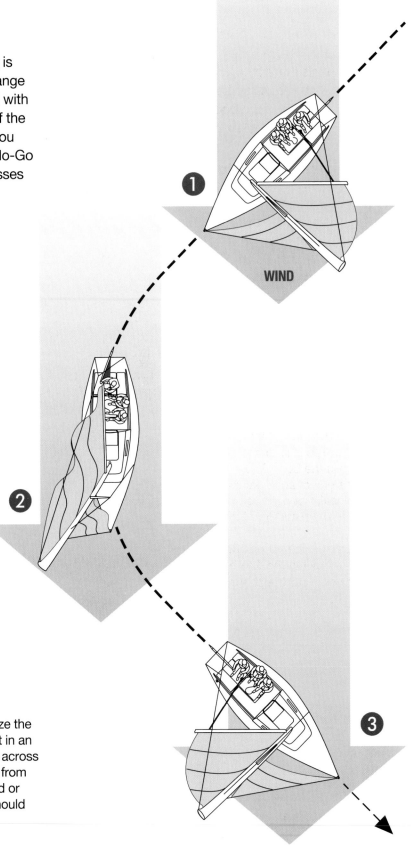

WIND

❶
❷
❸

DANGEROUS UNCONTROLLED JIBES!

The boat in this illustration is going through an uncontrolled jibe, forgetting sheet in the mainsail. The force of the boom rapidly swinging across the cockpit can break rigging or hit a crew member. In illustrations ❷ and ❸ it is still possible to avoid the uncontrolled jibe if the helmsman heads up to the original course in illustration ❶.
The key thing to do if the uncontrolled jibe occurs ❹ is to quickly duck under the boom's path. *The alert sailor should shout out a warning, "Duck!"*

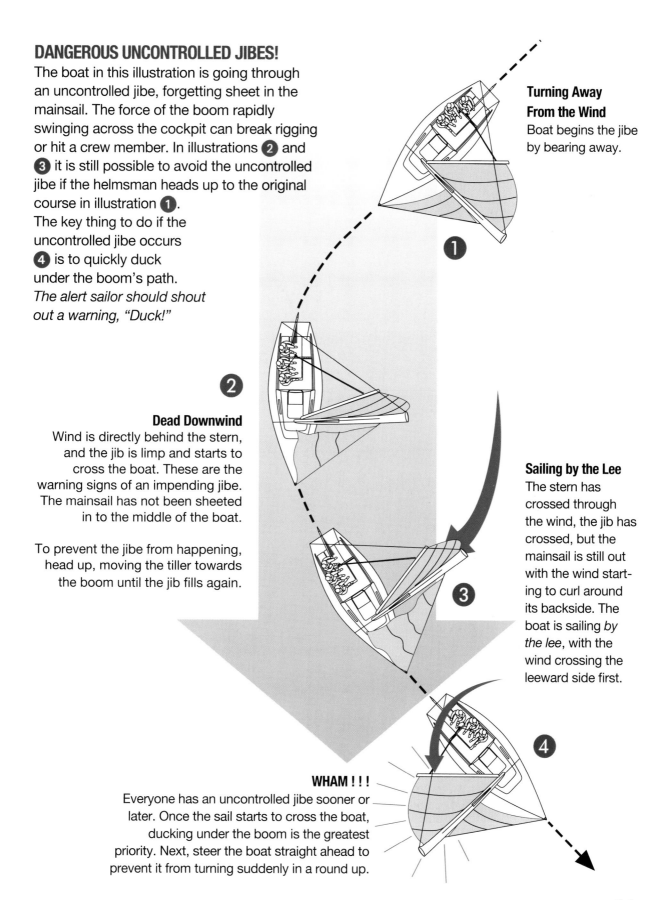

Turning Away From the Wind
Boat begins the jibe by bearing away.

Dead Downwind
Wind is directly behind the stern, and the jib is limp and starts to cross the boat. These are the warning signs of an impending jibe. The mainsail has not been sheeted in to the middle of the boat.

To prevent the jibe from happening, head up, moving the tiller towards the boom until the jib fills again.

Sailing by the Lee
The stern has crossed through the wind, the jib has crossed, but the mainsail is still out with the wind starting to curl around its backside. The boat is sailing *by the lee*, with the wind crossing the leeward side first.

WHAM ! ! !
Everyone has an uncontrolled jibe sooner or later. Once the sail starts to cross the boat, ducking under the boom is the greatest priority. Next, steer the boat straight ahead to prevent it from turning suddenly in a round up.

GETTING THERE AND RETURNING

Now, let's put everything you just learned together by sailing upwind, across the wind and downwind. Let's start by sailing *upwind* to a buoy with a series of *tacks*. Then, we'll sail across the wind on a reach to another buoy. After rounding the second buoy, we'll sail downwind using a series of *jibes*. Tacks are usually made at 90 degree angles. Jibes are usually made at much smaller angles.

Sailing Upwind

▶ Wind coming over the bow of boat.
▶ Sails are sheeted in all the way.
▶ Helmsman steers boat toward the wind as much as possible.
▶ Boat may sail a series of tacks to reach a destination.

Tip: Sailing upwind is also called *beating to windward*, or *beating*.

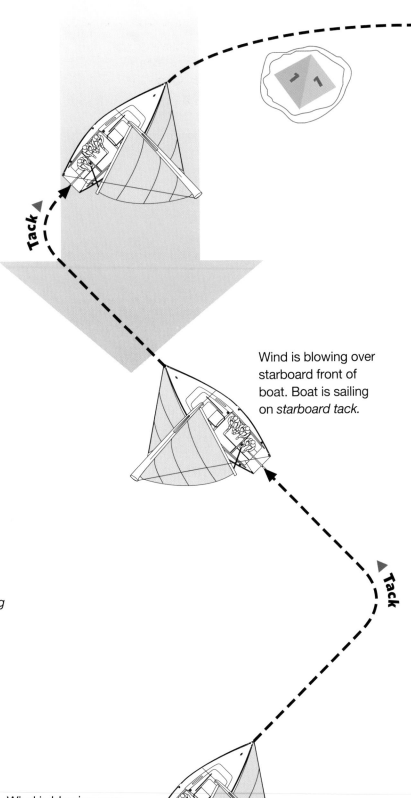

Wind is blowing over starboard front of boat. Boat is sailing on *starboard tack*.

Wind is blowing over port front of boat. Boat is sailing on *port tack*.

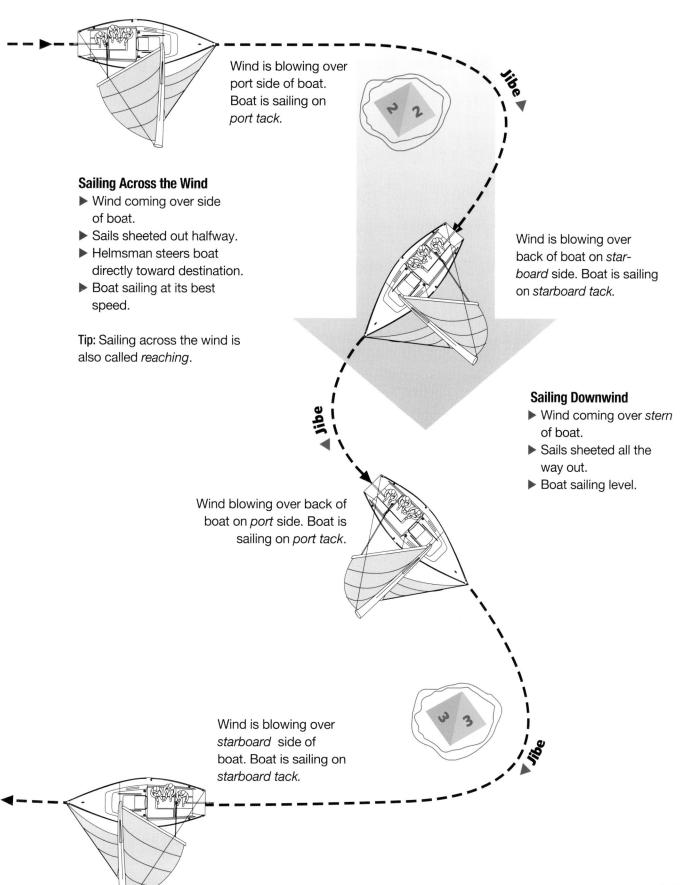

Wind is blowing over port side of boat. Boat is sailing on *port tack.*

Sailing Across the Wind

▶ Wind coming over side of boat.
▶ Sails sheeted out halfway.
▶ Helmsman steers boat directly toward destination.
▶ Boat sailing at its best speed.

Tip: Sailing across the wind is also called *reaching*.

Wind is blowing over back of boat on *star-board* side. Boat is sailing on *starboard tack.*

Sailing Downwind

▶ Wind coming over *stern* of boat.
▶ Sails sheeted all the way out.
▶ Boat sailing level.

Wind blowing over back of boat on *port* side. Boat is sailing on *port tack*.

Wind is blowing over *starboard* side of boat. Boat is sailing on *starboard tack.*

WARM WEATHER DRESSING

If you want to enjoy sailing, you've got to be comfortable. Preparation is the key, so put together a sailing gear bag for yourself with clothing and gear that will protect you and make you feel at ease in all weather conditions. Whether it's cloudy or sunny, protect yourself with sunscreen, using Sun Protection Factor (SPF) 15 or higher. You can get burned even on a cloudy day, especially with the sun's rays reflecting off the water.

Life jackets, are essential. They must be carried on all boats, and US Sailing recommends they be worn at all times, and especially on cold windy days.

Type I   Type II   Type III   Type V

The offshore life jacket, or **Type I**, is very buoyant, but bulky. It is designed for moderately heavy seas and will keep an unconscious person's head face up. The Near-Shore Buoyant Vest, or **Type II**, is less bulky but not as buoyant as the Type I. Common to many boats, the Type II turns some unconscious people to a face-up position. The vest type, or **Type III**, is more comfortable and allows for easier swimming than the other two, but is not designed to keep a person' s face out of the water. **Type V inflatable** is the least restrictive life jacket. It is worn as a vest or as a belt pack.

Sunglasses cut down the glare from the water and ease eye strain. Attach "keepers" (a cord around your neck) to your sunglasses to keep from losing them overboard.

A light-colored, knit **cotton or synthetic shirt** will keep you cool and protect your neck and upper arms from sunburn. Consider wearing a rash guard for extra protection.

Watches tend to take a beating on a boat. Leave a fine timepiece at home and wear an affordable, water resistant model on the water.

Sailing gloves (with cutaway finger tips) protect your hands and allow dexterity to work on delicate tasks.

Most **deck shoes** have "razor cut" soles with thin slits that open as the foot is flexed, allowing the shoe to grip a wet deck. Unless you like scrubbing decks, make sure your soles are non-marking.

10% of body heat escapes from the top of the head. A weather-proof hat will help keep you dry. Tie it on so it doesn't get lost overboard. The combination of a **knit ski cap** under the hood of your foul-weather jacket will keep you both warm and dry.

A **nylon-fleece jacket** with a tall collar will keep you warm and protect your neck from wind and spray. When worn over a turtleneck and sweater, you will be warm enough for most sailing situations.

Full-fingered **sailing gloves** make it easier to hold onto *lines* (ropes) and tiller on a chilly day.

Loose-fitting long pants over long underwear is usually enough to keep most people's legs warm. If you're still cold, you can wear your foul-weather gear pants on top. Loose pants also allow easier movement.

COOL WEATHER DRESSING

Cold, wet weather offers more challenges to staying comfortable. Remember, just because a day looks dry and warm in the morning doesn't mean it's going to stay that way. Be prepared for a change in the weather, and carry your gear with you. The best defense against cold weather is a layered approach, from long underwear to a long-sleeved shirt and pants to a sweater or fleece pull over to an insulated jacket to foul-weather gear. Keeping your hands, feet, and head warm with gloves, socks, and a hat is essential for comfort.

The protection provided by the **foul-weather gear** keeps sailing pleasurable even in wet conditions. Two-piece foul-weather gear (pants and a jacket) is more versatile than a one-piece jump-suit. There are often weather conditions in which you will want to wear only the jacket or only the pants.

In selecting gear, make sure it:
► Fits comfortably with enough room for movement and for extra clothes underneath
► Has flaps covering zippers and pockets
► Has velcro or elastic closures at the ankles and wrists
► Has abundant pockets
► Has a hood

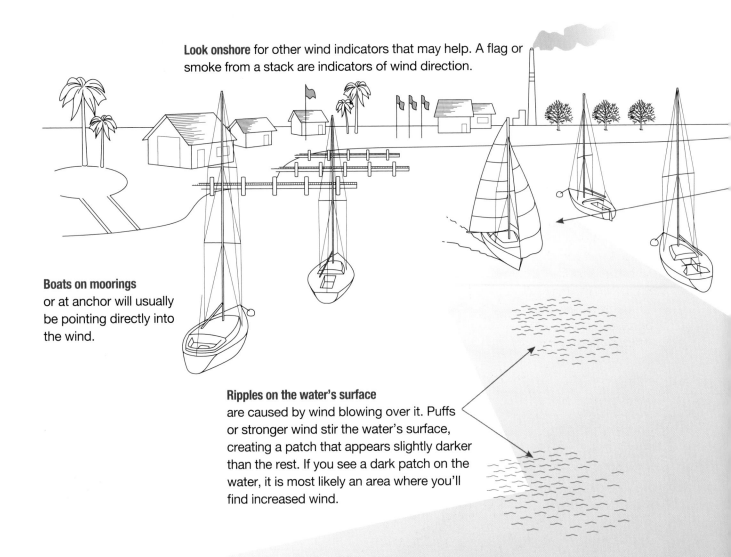

Look onshore for other wind indicators that may help. A flag or smoke from a stack are indicators of wind direction.

Boats on moorings or at anchor will usually be pointing directly into the wind.

Ripples on the water's surface are caused by wind blowing over it. Puffs or stronger wind stir the water's surface, creating a patch that appears slightly darker than the rest. If you see a dark patch on the water, it is most likely an area where you'll find increased wind.

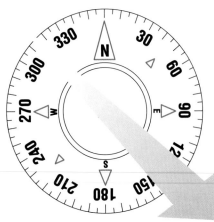

Wind direction is described by the direction from which it comes. A westerly wind is one that comes out of the West and blows toward the East. The wind on this compass rose is coming from a direction between North and West. It would be called a Northwest wind (or a Northwester).

"READING" THE WIND

Obviously you need wind to sail. You also need to know the direction of the wind. Out on the water you might have a nice breeze blowing, but if you don't know its direction, you won't know how to set your sails or steer your course. There are many clues, both on land and water, which you can use to tell which way the wind is blowing.

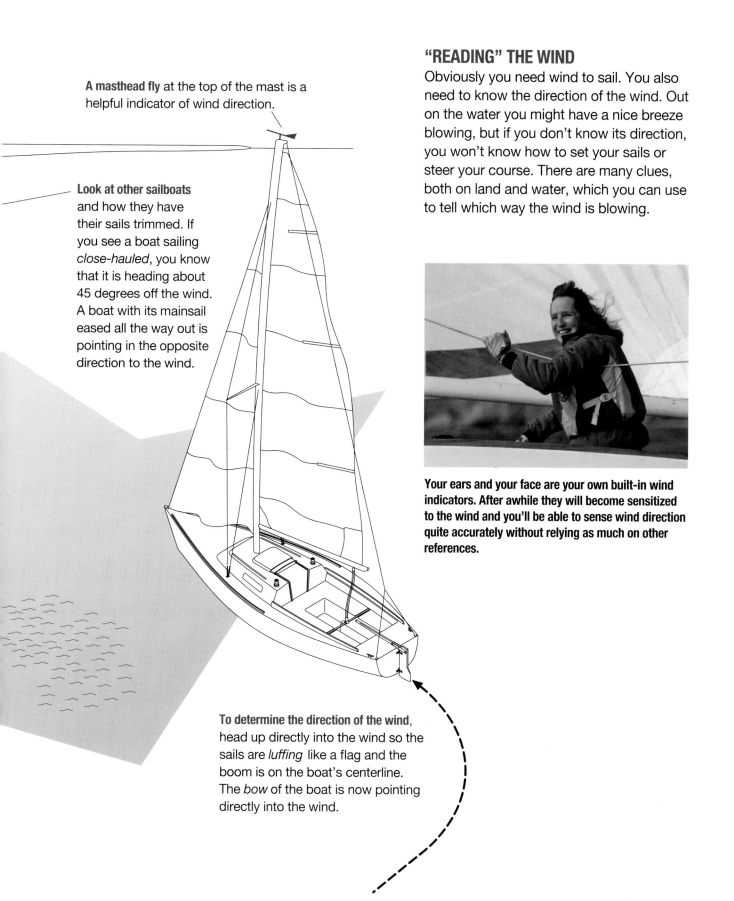

A masthead fly at the top of the mast is a helpful indicator of wind direction.

Look at other sailboats and how they have their sails trimmed. If you see a boat sailing *close-hauled*, you know that it is heading about 45 degrees off the wind. A boat with its mainsail eased all the way out is pointing in the opposite direction to the wind.

Your ears and your face are your own built-in wind indicators. After awhile they will become sensitized to the wind and you'll be able to sense wind direction quite accurately without relying as much on other references.

To determine the direction of the wind, head up directly into the wind so the sails are *luffing* like a flag and the boom is on the boat's centerline. The *bow* of the boat is now pointing directly into the wind.

PARTS OF A SAIL

Sails on modern sailboats are triangular, and the three corners and the three edges of the sail all have different names. Sails are raised by a line called a halyard attached to the top corner.

Edges of a Sail

▶ The bottom edge of a sail is called the **foot**. The foot of a mainsail is attached to the *boom*, while the *foot* of a jib is unattached.

▶ The forward edge of a sail is called the **luff**. On the jib the *luff* is attached (usually by *hanks*) to the forestay. The *luff* of the mainsail is attached to the *mast*.

▶ The back (*after*) edge of each of the sails is called the **leech**. It is not attached to the rig, but has battens installed for support.

Halyards

Halyards are used to raise and lower the sails, and are often led inside the mast.

▶ The **jib halyard** runs over an internal pulley (*sheave*) in the front of the mast.

▶ The **main halyard** runs over the *sheave* on the back side of the top of the mast.

Corners of a Sail

▶ Both jib and mainsail are attached to the rig at their lower forward corners. This corner of the sail is called the **tack**.

▶ The lower back corner of each sail is called the **clew**. The *jib sheets* are attached to the clew of the jib, and the *outhaul* is attached to the clew of the mainsail.

▶ The top corner of the sails is called the **head**, and is attached to the *halyard*. The head is the corner with the smallest angle of the three corners.

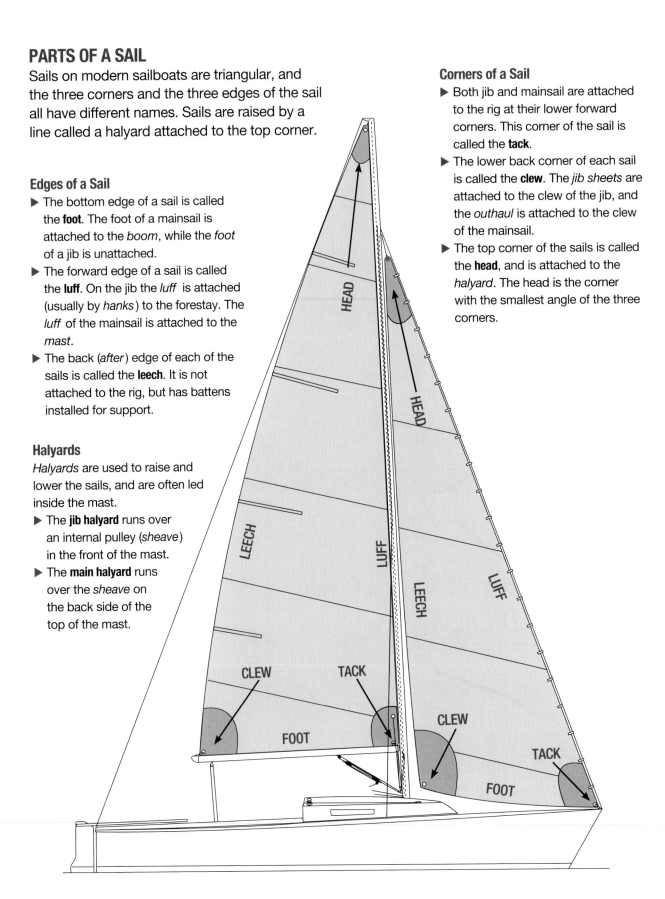

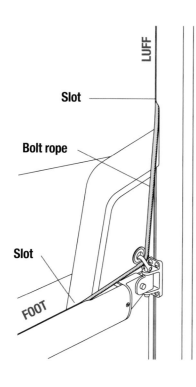

Slot

Bolt rope

Slot

LUFF

FOOT

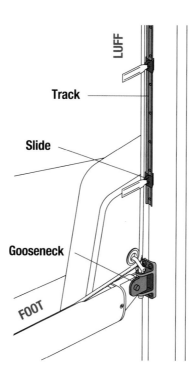

Track

Slide

Gooseneck

LUFF

FOOT

Gooseneck: A fitting capable of moving in all directions that connects the boom to the mast. This is where the *tack* of the mainsail is usually attached.

The *luff* and *foot* of the mainsail are attached to the mast and boom by either a **slot** (left) or a **track** (mast on right). The sail is made with either a *bolt rope* or *plastic slugs* that fit into the slot, or metal fittings that slide on the track.

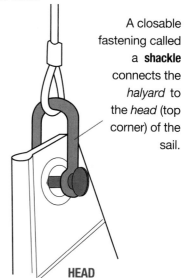

A closable fastening called a **shackle** connects the *halyard* to the *head* (top corner) of the sail.

HEAD

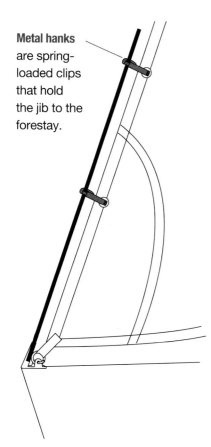

Metal hanks are spring-loaded clips that hold the jib to the forestay.

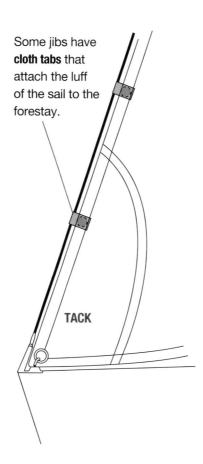

Some jibs have **cloth tabs** that attach the luff of the sail to the forestay.

TACK

RIGGING THE SAILS

Before leaving the dock the sails must be properly attached and raised. Sail controls such as an outhaul, vang, downhaul, or Cunningham may need to be adjusted before getting underway. Some boats are now fitted with a roller furler unit, a mechanical system to roll up a jib around the headstay. Roller furler jibs are always stored in the rolled-up position.

Rigging the Jib:

1. Fasten the *tack* of the jib to the proper fitting at the bow.
2. Starting with the bottom fastener, attach the *luff* of the jib onto the forestay without twisting the sail.
3. Attach the *jib halyard shackle* to the head of the jib. Check that the *halyard* is not wrapped around the forestay, shrouds or mast.
5. Secure the jib sheets to the *clew* of the jib using *bowline knots*. Depending on the type of boat you are sailing the jib sheets may pass inside or outside of the *shrouds*, then through the *fairleads*, and to the cockpit. Tie a stopper knot (usually a *figure-8 knot*) into the ends of the sheets in the cockpit.

Make sure all halyard shackles are fastened securely.

Rigging the Mainsail:

1. Attach the entire *foot* to the boom by inserting the *clew* of the sail into the forward end of the boom slot, pulling it along the boom.
2. Attach the *tack* of the sail to the *gooseneck*.
3. Connect the *Cunningham* but don't tighten.
4. Attach and tighten the outhaul to tension the foot of the main. Cleat the outhaul line.
5. Attach the luff to the mast, making sure it's not twisted. If it is connected by metal or fiberglass slides, feed them onto the track, and make sure they are all attached. If it uses a *bolt rope*, slide the head into the slot on the mast.
6. Attach the *main halyard shackle* and remove any slack to keep it from snagging a spreader and prevent the head from slipping out of the slot.
7. If *battens* have been removed, insert them before raising the sail. The more flexible end, usually thinner or tapered, should be inserted into the pocket first.

Before you hoist the mainsail, remove slack from the halyard to keep it from tangling in the rigging.

Tie jib sheets into the clew with bowline knots (see p.58).

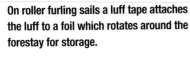

On roller furling sails a luff tape attaches the luff to a foil which rotates around the forestay for storage.

HOISTING THE SAILS

Before hoisting your sails, the boat should be pointed into the wind. The mainsail is usually hoisted first, as it will help keep the boat's bow into the wind (and No-Go Zone) until you are ready to cast off. If departing from the windward side of a dock, it may be preferable to hoist the jib first, sail away, and then hoist the mainsail once clear of the dock.

Snug up your outhaul before raising the sail. It's harder to do once the mainsail is hoisted and the boom is moving in the wind.

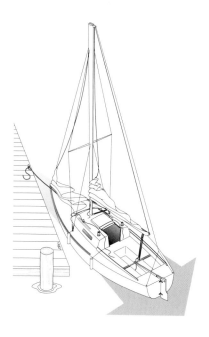

Hoisting the Mainsail:

1. Tighten the outhaul.
2. Loosen the Cunningham and/or downhaul.
3. Loosen the mainsheet and any reefing lines and remove any sail ties.
4. Tighten the traveler controls.
5. Release the boom vang.
6. Check the halyard to make sure it's clear, then hoist away.
7. Look up the mast to check that the sail is going up smoothly.
8. Allow the sail to *luff* so it will go up more easily.
9. Wrap the halyard around a *winch* if it becomes difficult to hold — be very careful when using a winch handle, it has the power to break something.
10. Cleat and coil the halyard.

Make sure the mainsheet and jib sheets are loose and free to run. This allows the sails to move freely in the wind so the boat doesn't start sailing at the dock!

You should now have both sails up and luffing with the boat aimed directly into the wind. The boat is still secured to the dock.

Hoisting the Jib:

1. Everyone should clear the foredeck so they are not hit by the sail as it flaps in the wind.
2. Make sure both the halyard and the jib sheets are clear and untangled.
3. Make sure the sheets are in the cockpit and free to run.
4. Raise the sail with the jib halyard. Finish hoisting by using a winch to properly tension the luff as necessary.
5. Secure and coil the halyard.

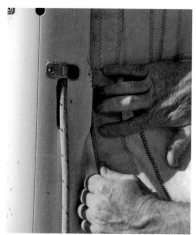

Feeding the mainsail luff into the slot of the mast as it is raised helps keep the sail from jamming in the slot.

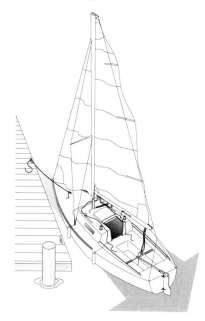

SAIL CONTROLS

The sail controls of a sailboat (running rigging) allow you to adjust the position and shape of the sails in response to changes in course, wind direction and wind strength. Each sail adjustment involves a system of components. For example, trimming the jib involves using the jib sheet, the fairleads, and winches. Let's take a quick look at the sail control components found on most sailboats.

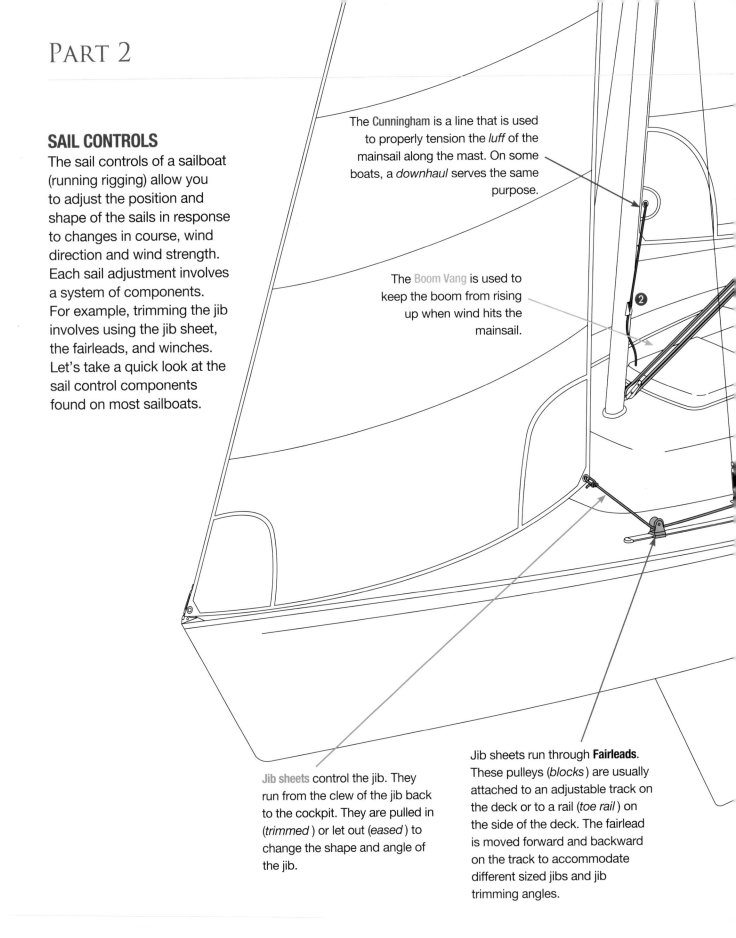

The **Cunningham** is a line that is used to properly tension the *luff* of the mainsail along the mast. On some boats, a *downhaul* serves the same purpose.

The **Boom Vang** is used to keep the boom from rising up when wind hits the mainsail.

Jib sheets control the jib. They run from the clew of the jib back to the cockpit. They are pulled in (*trimmed*) or let out (*eased*) to change the shape and angle of the jib.

Jib sheets run through **Fairleads**. These pulleys (*blocks*) are usually attached to an adjustable track on the deck or to a rail (*toe rail*) on the side of the deck. The fairlead is moved forward and backward on the track to accommodate different sized jibs and jib trimming angles.

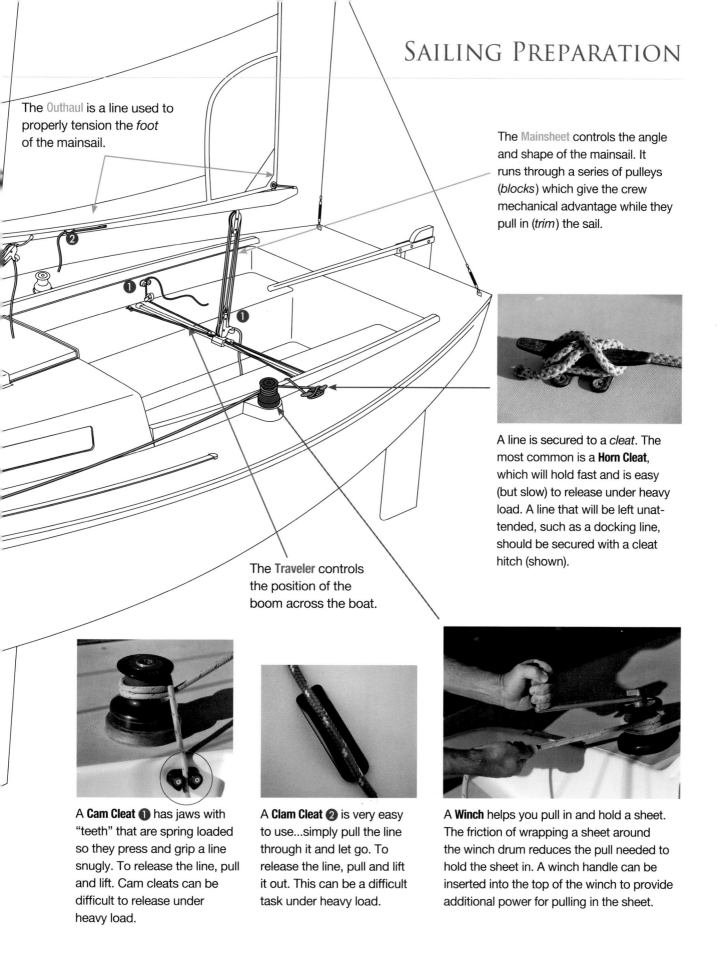

The Outhaul is a line used to properly tension the *foot* of the mainsail.

The Mainsheet controls the angle and shape of the mainsail. It runs through a series of pulleys (*blocks*) which give the crew mechanical advantage while they pull in (*trim*) the sail.

A line is secured to a *cleat*. The most common is a **Horn Cleat**, which will hold fast and is easy (but slow) to release under heavy load. A line that will be left unattended, such as a docking line, should be secured with a cleat hitch (shown).

The Traveler controls the position of the boom across the boat.

A **Cam Cleat** ❶ has jaws with "teeth" that are spring loaded so they press and grip a line snugly. To release the line, pull and lift. Cam cleats can be difficult to release under heavy load.

A **Clam Cleat** ❷ is very easy to use...simply pull the line through it and let go. To release the line, pull and lift it out. This can be a difficult task under heavy load.

A **Winch** helps you pull in and hold a sheet. The friction of wrapping a sheet around the winch drum reduces the pull needed to hold the sheet in. A winch handle can be inserted into the top of the winch to provide additional power for pulling in the sheet.

LEAVING THE DOCK

Like learning how to park a car, learning how to leave or return to a dock can make beginning sailors nervous. With a little forethought and only basic sailing skills you can leave and return to a dock with confidence. Boats and docks are large objects and the safety of your crew should be the foremost thought when departing or arriving at a dock.

First decide how you will leave the dock, then explain your departure plan to the crew members. Make sure everyone knows what they should do and when. In both examples shown here, the boat is pointed into the wind (No-Go Zone) and must be turned out of the zone to sail away from the dock. In the example above, there is an open sailing area to the left of the dock. In the bottom example the boat will have to be backed out of the slip before it can be turned out of the No-Go Zone.

In preparation for leaving the dock, make sure the fenders are positioned to protect the boat while leaving the dock.

Leaving a Dock

1 Your sails are up and luffing as you are tied to the dock pointed into the wind. A crew member is on the dock to handle the docklines. Release the bow line first, and then step aboard at the shrouds or stern while helping to push the boat away from the dock.

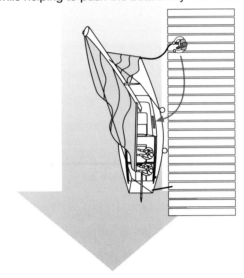

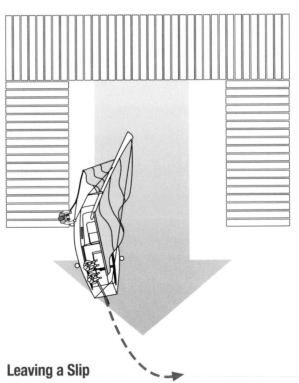

Leaving a Slip

1 The crew on the dock carefully guides the boat by hand around the end of the dock.

2 Sheet in the jib on the dock (right) side until the sail becomes backwinded and the boat slowly rotates out of the No-Go Zone. Then release the stern line either from a position on the boat or dock. Double the line back to the boat so it can be released. To double the stern line, undo the cleat on the dock and loop the line around the base of the cleat, returning the tail end to a crew member on board.

3 Finally, sheet in the jib on the other side, and trim the mainsail, to propel you forward. Enjoy your sail!

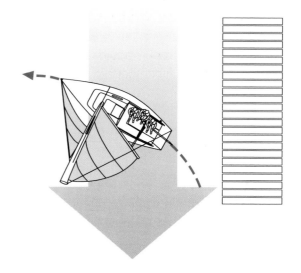

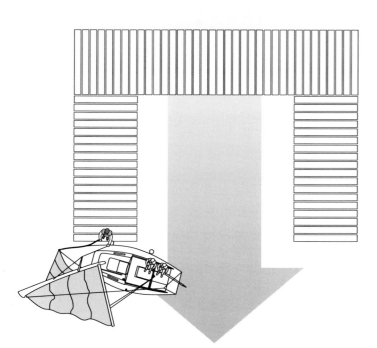

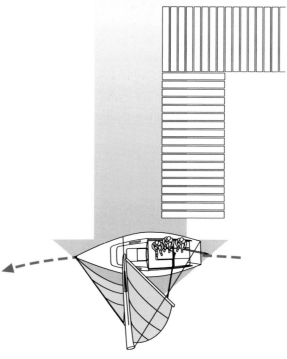

2 The bow is maneuvered past the end of the dock. The boat is guided alongside the dock towards the sailing area. The crew pushes off from the dock and steps on the boat holding onto the shrouds.

3 The sails are sheeted in, and fenders and docklines are stowed.

CREW POSITION

A small sailboat is relatively light, so the positioning of a helmsman and crew is critical to how the boat handles. The crew not only trim sails, but also help to balance the boat. Note how everyone is positioned on the windward (high) side of the boat. When the crew sits farther out on the rail (side), their weight helps counteract the boat's tendency to heel when the wind pushes against the sails. This is important, because excessive heel slows the boat and makes it harder to steer.

Crew Responsibilities

The crew are in charge of trimming and easing the jib sheet and mainsheet. They will be the first to cross the cockpit during a *tack*, and will snug up the sheet not being used (*lazy sheet*) so it will be ready to trim for the next tack.

Helmsman Responsibilities

The helmsman should be seated just forward of the tiller, holding the tiller with the hand farthest aft. On a two-person boat, he or she holds the mainsheet in the other hand and adjusts sail trim or course as needed. In a three-person crew, the middle crew usually handles the mainsheet and the helmsman only steers.

During tacks and jibes, the boom crosses over the cockpit. The helmsman and crew must first duck under the boom and cross over to the other side of the boat.

STEERING

Using a tiller to steer the boat is simple. A common rule of thumb when you begin sailing is to push or pull the tiller away from the direction you want to turn. If you want to turn left, push or pull the tiller right, and vice versa. After a short while, using a tiller will become instinctive.

(Follow sequence from bottom ❶ to top ❸)

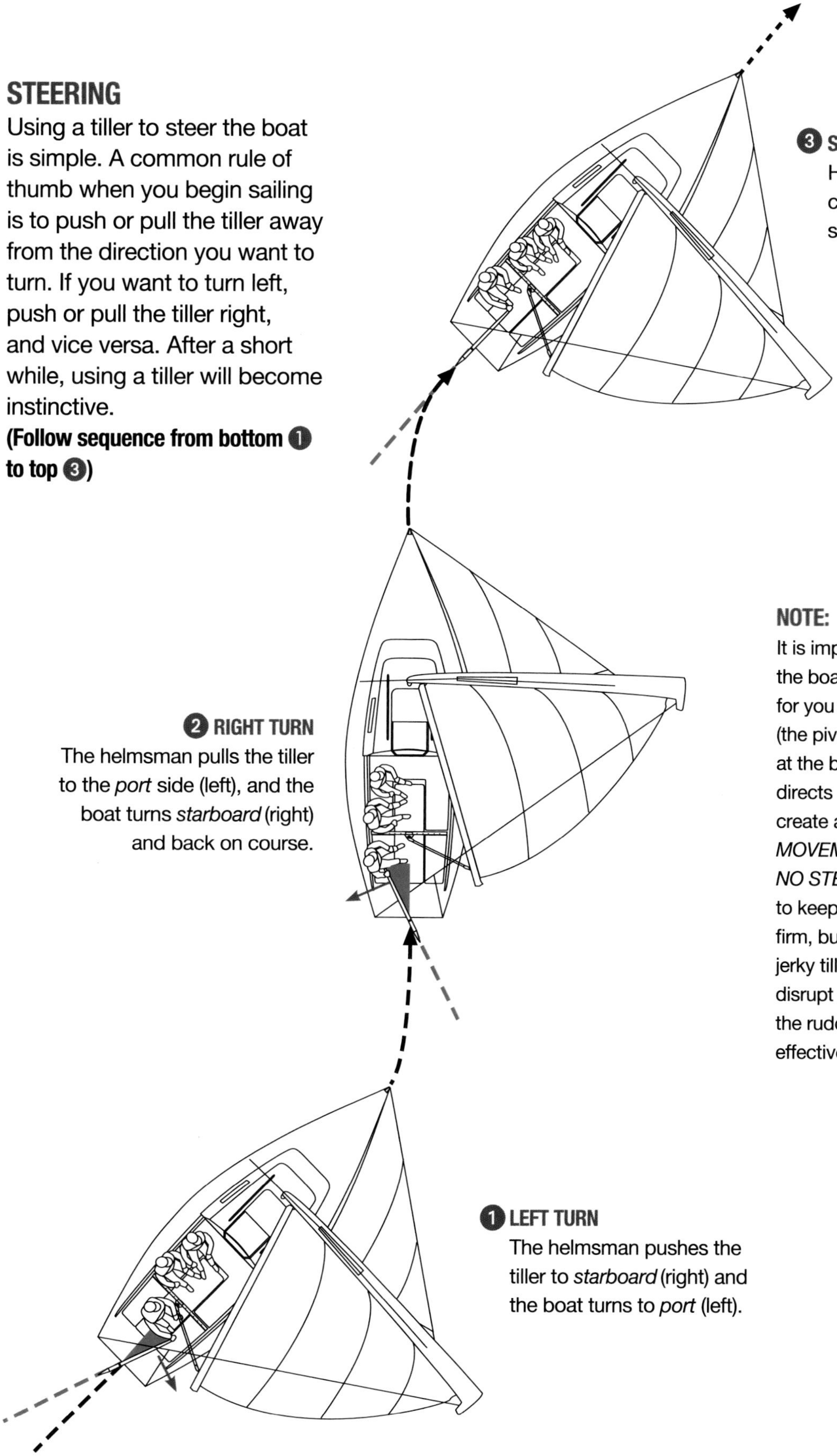

❸ STRAIGHT AHEAD
Here the helmsman has centered the tiller and is sailing a straight course.

❷ RIGHT TURN
The helmsman pulls the tiller to the *port* side (left), and the boat turns *starboard* (right) and back on course.

NOTE:
It is important to know that the boat must be moving for you to steer. The *rudder* (the pivoting underwater foil at the back of the boat) re-directs the flow of water to create a steering force. *NO MOVEMENT...NO FLOW... NO STEERING FORCE!* Try to keep the steering motion firm, but smooth. Herky, jerky tiller movements can disrupt water flow around the rudder and reduce its effectiveness.

❶ LEFT TURN
The helmsman pushes the tiller to *starboard* (right) and the boat turns to *port* (left).

STARTING AND STOPPING

A sailboat can start and stop by using its
sails, much like using the accelerator on a car.
Sheeting-in a sail to proper trim is like stepping
on the accelerator. Easing the sail out and letting
it *luff* is like taking your foot off the gas. With the
sails luffing, the boat will coast to a stop.

Stop
Boat is stopped in the water with
its sheets eased out and its sails
completely *luffing*.

Start
Sheeting in the sails to their proper
trim gets the boat moving.

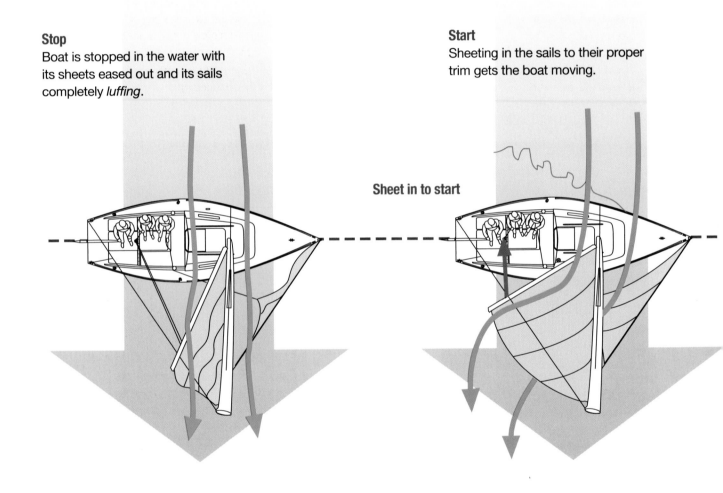

Sheet in to start

Stop

To stop the boat the sails are eased out until they are luffing. The boat then coasts to a stop.

Head up into No-Go Zone to stop

To stop the boat head up directly into the *No-Go Zone*. The sails luff completely and the boat stops. To stop the boat more quickly, a crew member pushes (*backs*) the mainsail against the wind (shown).

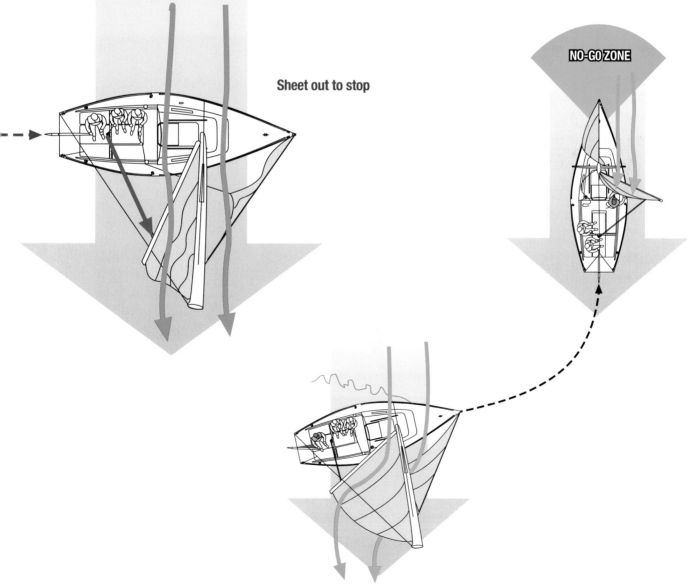

Sheet out to stop

NO-GO ZONE

JIB AND MAINSAIL TRIM

Sail trim is one of the most important skills in sailing, but because the wind is invisible, it can sometimes be difficult to judge whether your sails are trimmed properly. A very helpful way to detect wind flow around your sails (and adjust your sails or change course accordingly) is with *telltales*.

How Telltales Work

Telltales are pieces of yarn or sail cloth attached near the *luff* of the sail.

▶ If the *windward* (closest to the direction from which the wind is coming) telltale is fluttering, either sheet in the jib toward the telltale or turn the boat away from the telltale (bear away) until it stops fluttering and flows smoothly.

▶ If both telltales stream straight back, it means the wind is flowing smoothly over both sides of the sail.

▶ If the *leeward* (farthest away from the wind's direction) telltale is fluttering, sheet out the sail toward the telltale or turn the boat away from the telltale (head up) until it flows smoothly.

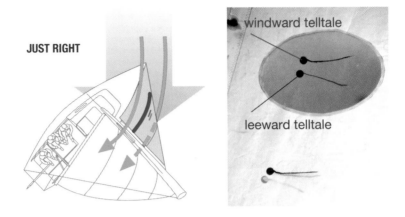

JUST RIGHT

Air flow is smooth on both sides of the jib, and the telltales are both streaming back.

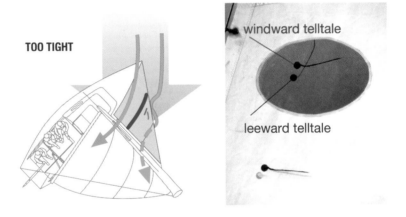

TOO TIGHT

This jib is sheeted in too tight. Air flow is turbulent on the outside (leeward) side of the sail as indicated by the fluttering telltale. Ease the jib sheet out or head up to get smooth air flow.

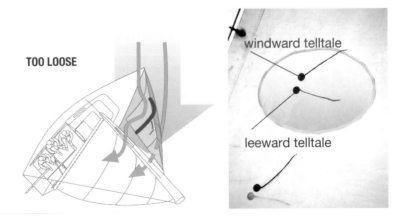

TOO LOOSE

This telltale on side closest to the wind (windward) is fluttering, indicating turbulence on that side of the sail. Sheet in the jib or bear away until the telltale stops fluttering.

JUST RIGHT

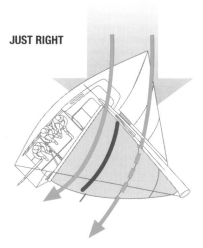

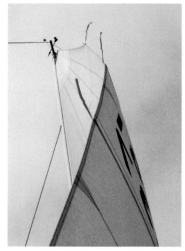

This mainsail is sheeted just right. The air flow is smooth on both sides of the sail, and the telltales on the leech are streaming back.

TOO TIGHT

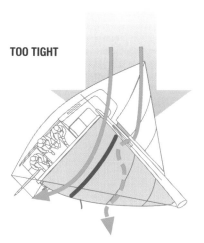

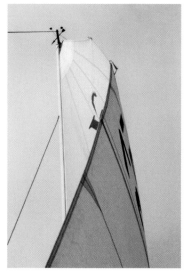

This mainsail is sheeted in too tightly. Air flow is turbulent on the outside (leeward side) of the sail as indicated by the fluttering telltale. Ease the mainsheet out to get smooth air flow. Many beginning sailors tend to trim mainsails too tight. Remember the saying,"When in doubt, let it out!"

TOO LOOSE
luff "bubble"

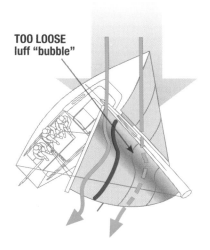

The mainsail here is trimmed too loose. Turbulent flow is indicated by a backing on the forward edge of the mainsail (luff "bubble").

SAILING IN THE GROOVE

As you learn to sail close to the wind, you will develop a technique called "sailing in the groove." The *groove* is an invisible sailing angle where your boat is making the best progress toward the wind (*to windward*). Sails will be trimmed in for close hauled and the boat is steered to the perfect angle to the wind. Finding the groove and staying there can be a bit of a challenge at first, but sailors soon learn how to "feel it" when their boat is in the groove. The best references are your boat's speed, how much it tips (*angle of heel*) and the telltales on the jib.

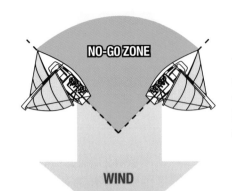

The No-Go Zone extends about 45 degrees off both sides of the eye of the wind.

Telltales stream back when wind flow is smooth and flutter upward when flow is turbulent.

What is "The Groove"
Experienced helmsmen don't sail a perfectly straight course upwind. They subtly "snake" a course along the edge of the No-Go Zone—first sailing closer to the wind to see if the sails are on the verge of luffing, then heading back away from the wind to fill the sails with wind. This technique is called sailing in the groove.

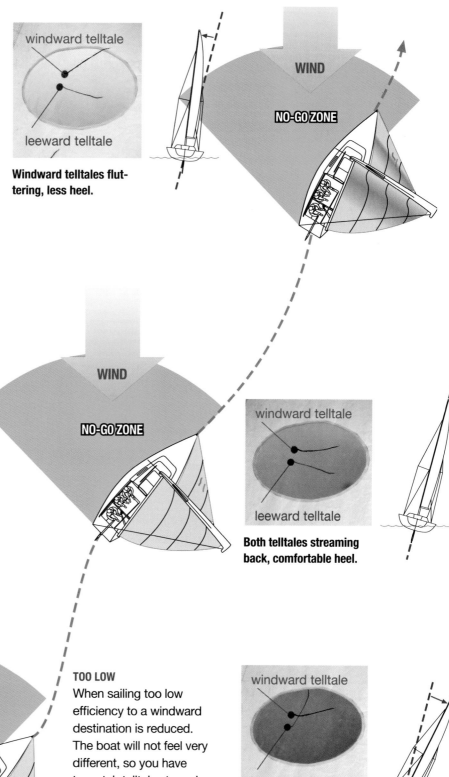

TOO HIGH

When sailing closer to the wind the boat heels less because there is less power in the sails. *The windward telltale will flutter.* At this point, smoothly steer back down away from the wind until the jib stops luffing and you feel your boat speed pick up again.

windward telltale
leeward telltale

Windward telltales fluttering, less heel.

WIND

NO-GO ZONE

JUST RIGHT

With perfect sail trim on the edge of the no-go zone the sails are working to maintain upwind efficiency. If you carefully steer the boat a bit more toward the wind, until you see the jib start to *luff.* You will feel the boat start to slow down like the example at the top of the page.

WIND

NO-GO ZONE

windward telltale
leeward telltale

Both telltales streaming back, comfortable heel.

WIND

NO-GO ZONE

TOO LOW

When sailing too low efficiency to a windward destination is reduced. The boat will not feel very different, so you have to watch telltales to make course corrections. Head up until both telltales are streaming straight back.

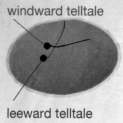

windward telltale
leeward telltale

Leeward telltales fluttering, too much heel.

43

PART 3

TACKING STEP-BY-STEP

You've already learned that tacking is changing a boat's direction by first turning the bow toward the wind (*heading up*), then through the wind and No-Go Zone, and away from the wind (*bearing away*) to a new direction. Also you've learned that whenever the bow turns through the wind, the sails will cross from one side to the other. Now you'll learn how to tack.

(Follow sequence from bottom ❶ to top ❹)

Tip: In sailing always remember that preparation and communication are key to the safety of your crew and enjoyment of your sail. These two factors are essential in all phases of the sport, including leaving the dock, anchoring, responding to emergencies, and tacking and jibing. Know what you are going to do and how you are going to do it. Talk to your crew…and listen.

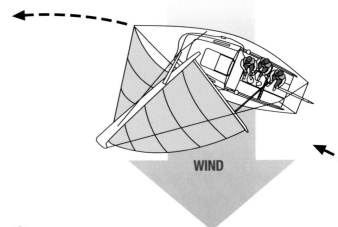

WIND

❹ **Tack Is Completed**

Once the tack is completed the helmsman centers the tiller and steers for the reference picked at the beginning of the tack. The crew adjust the mainsail and jib for the new direction. The jib sheets are then coiled and readied for the next tack.

❶ **Preparing to Tack**

The boat is on a beam reach with the wind coming over the *port* side of the boat. Helmsman checks for anything that might be in the way, selects a reference point to steer for after completion of the tack, and then calls out, "*Ready about!*" The crew checks to make sure the jib sheets are clear and ready to run out, then uncleats and holds the working jib sheet and gets ready to sheet in the lazy jib sheet before responding, "*Ready!*"

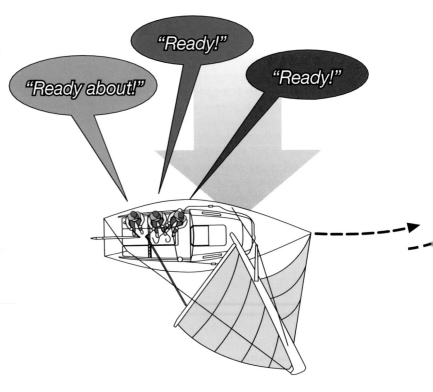

"Ready about!"   "Ready!"   "Ready!"

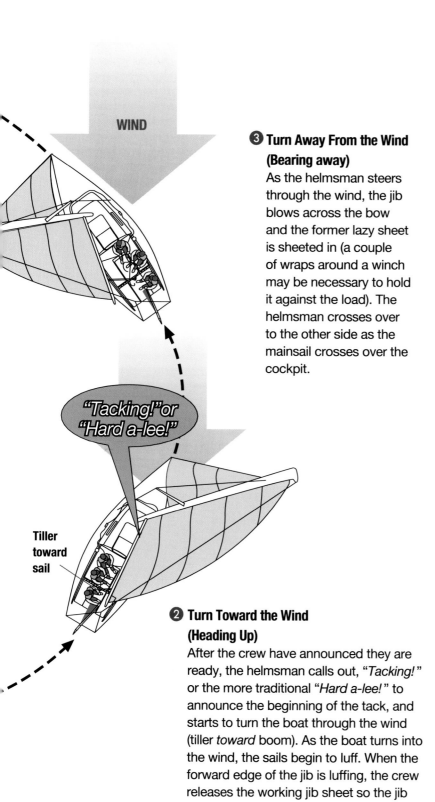

WIND

❸ Turn Away From the Wind (Bearing away)

As the helmsman steers through the wind, the jib blows across the bow and the former lazy sheet is sheeted in (a couple of wraps around a winch may be necessary to hold it against the load). The helmsman crosses over to the other side as the mainsail crosses over the cockpit.

"Tacking!" or *"Hard a-lee!"*

Tiller toward sail

❷ Turn Toward the Wind (Heading Up)

After the crew have announced they are ready, the helmsman calls out, *"Tacking!"* or the more traditional *"Hard a-lee!"* to announce the beginning of the tack, and starts to turn the boat through the wind (tiller *toward* boom). As the boat turns into the wind, the sails begin to luff. When the forward edge of the jib is luffing, the crew releases the working jib sheet so the jib can cross over to the other side.

HEAVING-TO

If you want or need to stop sailing, for instance to check a chart, or relax for lunch, the best way is to heave-to. Heaving-to holds your position with the sails and rudder countering each other as the boat drifts forward and to leeward (*downwind*). Always check that you have plenty of room to drift downwind before heaving-to.

❶ To heave-to, steer your boat so it is sailing close to the wind with the jib sheeted tightly.

❷ Tack the boat, but do not uncleat the jib sheet. The jib will become "backed."

❸ Ease the mainsail. Let the boat slow to a stop and move the tiller toward the boom and, after the boat has settled down, secure the tiller to leeward.

❹ Trim the mainsail so the boat lies at an upwind angle.

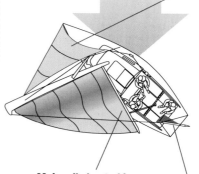

Jib aback

Mainsail sheeted in
You may need to trim the main differently on different boats. Experiment to find out what works on your boat.

Tiller tied to keep the boat on a constant angle to the wind

45

JIBING STEP-BY-STEP

As you have already learned, jibing is changing the direction of the boat while passing the stern through the wind. Again, preparing and communicating with your crew is essential for a smooth, controlled, and safe maneuver.

(Follow sequence from top ❶ to bottom ❹)

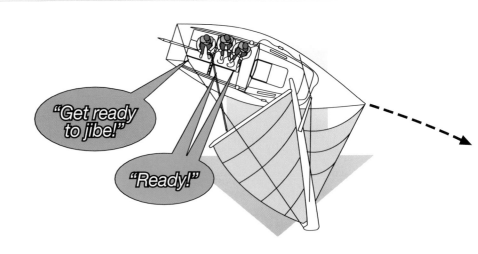

"Get ready to jibe!"

"Ready!"

❶ Preparing to Jibe

Helmsman checks wind direction and selects reference to steer for after completion of jibe, and then calls out, *"Get ready to jibe!"* The crew check the sheets to make sure they are ready to run out, and uncleat the working jib sheet and mainsheet before responding, *"Ready!"*

It is important to be aware of the boom crossing the boat and to keep your head down!

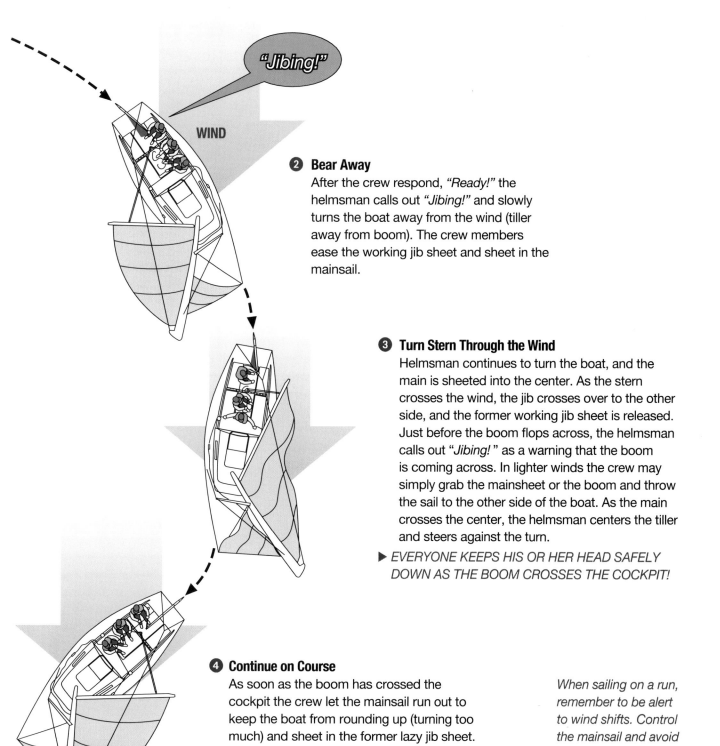

"Jibing!"

WIND

❷ Bear Away

After the crew respond, *"Ready!"* the helmsman calls out *"Jibing!"* and slowly turns the boat away from the wind (tiller away from boom). The crew members ease the working jib sheet and sheet in the mainsail.

❸ Turn Stern Through the Wind

Helmsman continues to turn the boat, and the main is sheeted into the center. As the stern crosses the wind, the jib crosses over to the other side, and the former working jib sheet is released. Just before the boom flops across, the helmsman calls out *"Jibing!"* as a warning that the boom is coming across. In lighter winds the crew may simply grab the mainsheet or the boom and throw the sail to the other side of the boat. As the main crosses the center, the helmsman centers the tiller and steers against the turn.

▶ *EVERYONE KEEPS HIS OR HER HEAD SAFELY DOWN AS THE BOOM CROSSES THE COCKPIT!*

❹ Continue on Course

As soon as the boom has crossed the cockpit the crew let the mainsail run out to keep the boat from rounding up (turning too much) and sheet in the former lazy jib sheet. The helmsman may steer the boat toward their destination.

When sailing on a run, remember to be alert to wind shifts. Control the mainsail and avoid an uncontrolled jibe.

RETURNING TO THE DOCK

Prepare the boat before returning to the dock. Have the fenders hung at the right height to safeguard the hull. Have the docklines attached properly to the boat and strung under the lifelines so they are ready to be used. Decide upon a plan for a controlled landing and inform the crew of their responsibilities. Be sure to have an escape plan if the landing isn't going well. Once you are ready to approach the dock, do it carefully.

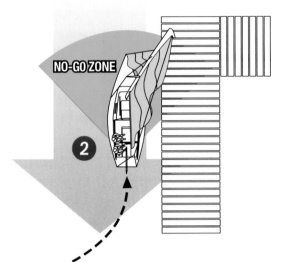

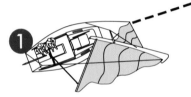

When nearing a side dock, ease out your sails on your approach to slow the boat ❶. As you come closer, steer up into the wind, letting the sails luff. Coast to a stop along the dock ❷. If the dock is short or has limited space, you will want to make your approach more slowly.

In making an approach to an upwind slip, ease the sails to slow your speed. Further decrease your speed, if necessary, by wiggling the boat back and forth on its course ❶. Once you are sure your speed is correct (fast enough to get you into the slip, but not fast enough to bang your bow), head into the slip ❷. If your speed is slightly high going into the slip, push the boom out to backwind the mainsail to help stop the boat.

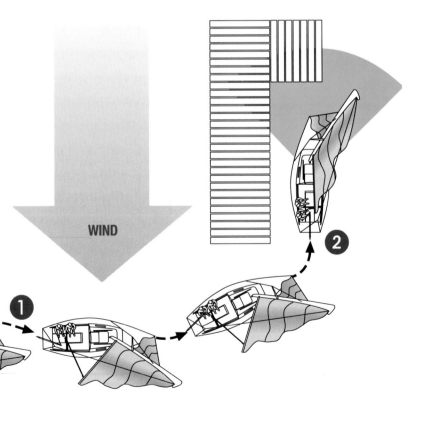

TYING UP AT THE DOCK

Crew members should step off the boat onto the dock. DO NOT JUMP! Falling on the dock or between the dock and the boat is a painful way to end your sail. Nothing other than a fender should be put between the boat and the dock.

Care should be taken while getting on and off a vessel. In general it is safer to use a shroud as a handhold while moving from the dock to the boat. Be careful of tripping while stepping over lifelines. Remember a boat may heel significantly when you embark or disembark the boat.

Docking Lines

▶ **Bow and stern lines** keep the boat close to the dock, but do not prevent it from surging forward or backward in the wind or waves.
▶ **Spring lines** keep the boat from moving forward and backward. Spring lines are referenced according to where they go from the cleat on the boat. For example, a spring line attached to the bow cleat that goes aft to the dock cleat is an aft spring line.

Cleated docking lines should always be secured with a cleat hitch.

Before you leave the boat, double check that the docklines are cleated securely with the right amount of tension. All cleated docking lines should be secured with a *cleat hitch* (see photo above).

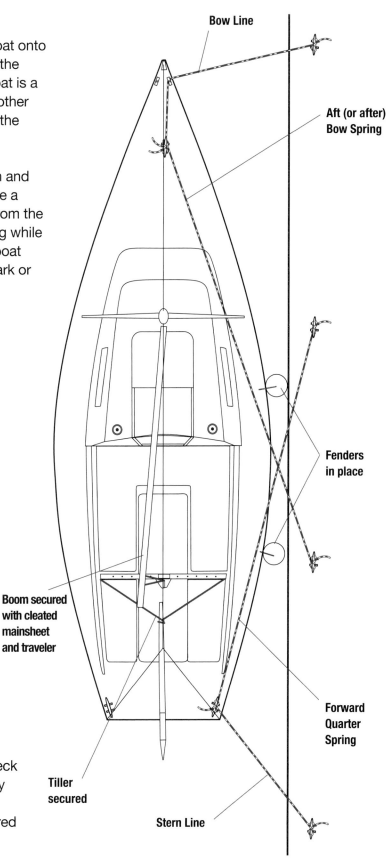

Bow Line

Aft (or after) Bow Spring

Fenders in place

Boom secured with cleated mainsheet and traveler

Forward Quarter Spring

Tiller secured

Stern Line

ADJUSTING SAIL SHAPE

Sails are not flat. They have curvature or shape built into them. The shape of a sail can be adjusted to give it more curvature (*fuller*) or less curvature (*flatter*). In light wind conditions, you want a full sail shape for greater power. As the wind increases, you want to *depower*, or make the sail flatter, to keep the boat under control and sailing well.

The Cunningham, named after its inventor, Briggs Cunningham, is a system used to tension the luff of the sail. This changes the shape of the sail and "depowers" it in higher winds. Tightening the outhaul helps to depower the bottom of the sail.

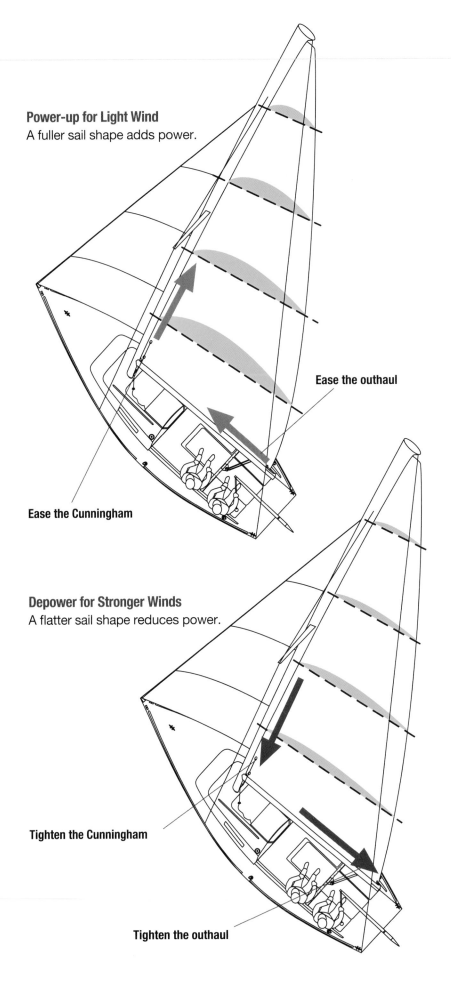

Power-up for Light Wind
A fuller sail shape adds power.

Ease the outhaul

Ease the Cunningham

Depower for Stronger Winds
A flatter sail shape reduces power.

Tighten the Cunningham

Tighten the outhaul

DEPOWERING SAILS

To keep stronger winds from overpowering the boat, you can ease out the sails to spill the excess wind (*depower*). Adjusting sail trim this way keeps a boat balanced and sailing at its best. As winds increase, or during gusts, *depower* your sails to help keep the boat in balance, decrease *heel* and make steering easier.

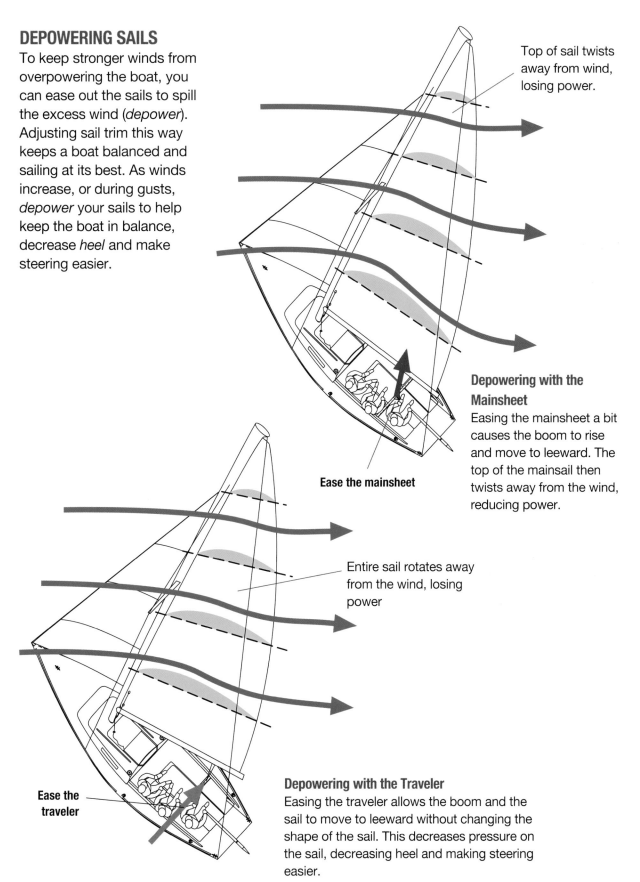

Top of sail twists away from wind, losing power.

Ease the mainsheet

Depowering with the Mainsheet

Easing the mainsheet a bit causes the boom to rise and move to leeward. The top of the mainsail then twists away from the wind, reducing power.

Entire sail rotates away from the wind, losing power

Ease the traveler

Depowering with the Traveler

Easing the traveler allows the boom and the sail to move to leeward without changing the shape of the sail. This decreases pressure on the sail, decreasing heel and making steering easier.

BALANCE

You can steer a boat with its sails instead of with the rudder because of a principle called *balance*. A sailboat is a collection of forces in motion, not all of which move the boat in the same direction. The forces generated by the sails move the boat to leeward as well as forward. The sideways motion is resisted by the keel and rudder, causing the boat to heel as it moves forward.

When all of these forces are *in balance*, the boat will sail forward in a straight line. When they are not, the boat will want to turn. The mainsail (pulling the stern to leeward) causes the boat to head up and the jib (pulling the bow to leeward) causes the boat to bear away. Because these forces are constantly changing and never exactly equal, small adjustments are needed to keep the boat on course. You can steer a boat by sheeting in or easing either the mainsail or jib. By doing so, you are consciously throwing the boat *in and out of balance*.

Understanding balance will help you control your boat. As your sailing skills improve, you will use this *principle of balance* to get the best performance out of your boat and execute more advanced maneuvers.

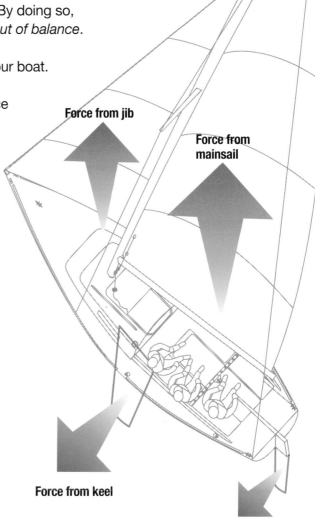

Force from jib

Force from mainsail

Force from keel

Force from rudder

TACKING ANGLES

You can reach an upwind destination in several ways. If the course is not obstructed, you can take a long zig and a long zag. In a channel or river you may need to use a series of short zig-zags to reach your destination. Sailing upwind requires course changes of about 90 degrees in most boats. A handy way to estimate your course after the next tack is to sight to windward directly off the side of the boat. If you can pick out a landmark, another sailboat, a cloud or other reference, it helps you get quickly oriented after a tack.

When tacking, your course options are unlimited, but the angle of your tacks is always the same: about 90 degrees.

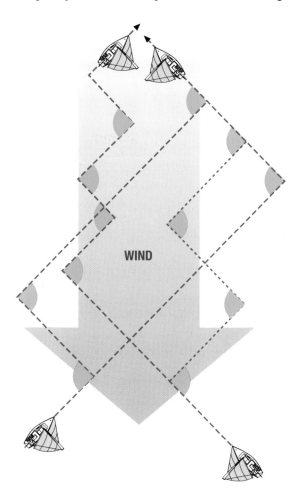

Tacking to an upwind destination is accomplished through a series of steps where you sail as close to the wind as possible.

JIBING ANGLES

Sailing with the wind, you can sail more directly toward your destination. Even though the wind is coming from behind, it is desirable to keep the wind coming over one side of the boat or the other, not directly behind.

Jibing angles are a lot more flexible and less structured than tacking angles. With the wind coming from behind, you do not have to contend with the No-Go Zone.

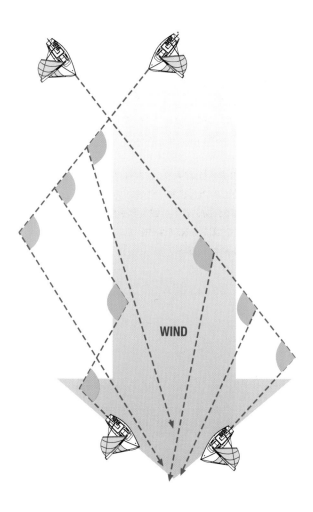

Similar to tacking upwind, you can either use just one or a series of jibes to head downwind.

WIND SHIFTS - UPWIND

Even the steadiest wind is constantly changing its direction (*shifting*). These changes range from almost unnoticable to major swings in direction. Wind shifts play a major role in how you sail *upwind*. When the wind shifts, it also swings your No-Go Zone toward one side or the other, affecting the course you are able to sail. You respond to these changes of wind direction by *heading up* or *bearing away*. In truly large wind shifts, you might even tack if the new tack will keep you sailing closer to your destination than your current one. (Follow sequence from bottom ❶ to top ❸)

❸ **Shift Forward**

The wind has *shifted forward* from the original direction. In order to keep from stopping in the No-Go Zone, the helmsman bears away until the boat is in the groove again. A wind shift that forces you to bear away is called a *header*.

❷ **Shift Aft**

The wind has *shifted aft*, also shifting the No-Go Zone and the groove. The helmsman recognizes the change in wind direction and heads *up*. A wind shift that allows you to head *up* is called a *lift*.

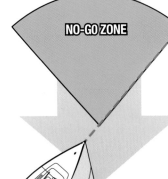

❶ A boat and its crew are sailing *upwind* in the groove.

WIND SHIFTS AND DISTANCE

Wind shifts (*headers* and *lifts*) do more than force you to change your course. They also shorten or lengthen the distance you will need to sail to reach a destination upwind. The example here shows how a header shortens the distance sailed to an upwind destination.

After being *headed* and then tacking, the helmsman of this boat made excellent time and progress to his destination.

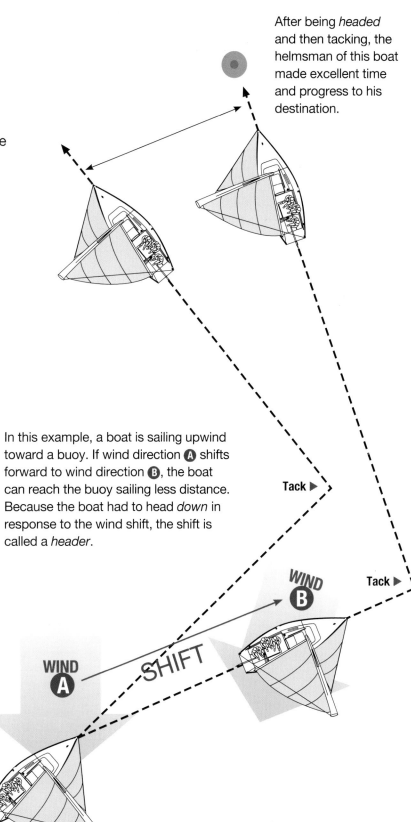

In this example, a boat is sailing upwind toward a buoy. If wind direction **A** shifts forward to wind direction **B**, the boat can reach the buoy sailing less distance. Because the boat had to head *down* in response to the wind shift, the shift is called a *header*.

Tack ▶

Tack ▶

WIND **B**

WIND **A**

SHIFT

Expert Tip:
When sailing upwind in shifty wind, always sail on the tack that has the closest angle to your destination. That way, you will be sailing the shortest distance (and the fastest course) to where you want to go.

MORE LEAVING AND RETURNING

You don't always leave and return to the dock under the ideal conditions described earlier. Awareness of the wind conditions, forethought, and knowledge of sail handling are necessary for approaching and departing docks, particularly when weather conditions offer a challenge.

Backward Departure

There may be times when you will have to sail the boat backward to leave the dock. Here's how to do it:

❶ Back away: push the boom out all the way in the direction you want the bow to turn (in this case to the left, or port) and hold out (*back*) the jib to the opposite direction. Center the tiller. The boat will sail backward.

❷ Turn out of the No-Go Zone: as soon as the boat has cleared the dock, turn the tiller toward the mainsail (the same direction you want the bow to turn) to turn out of the No-Go Zone.

❸ Sail away: when the boat has turned out of the No-Go Zone and is pointed in the desired direction, release the jib and sheet it in on the correct side, trim the mainsail and center the tiller.

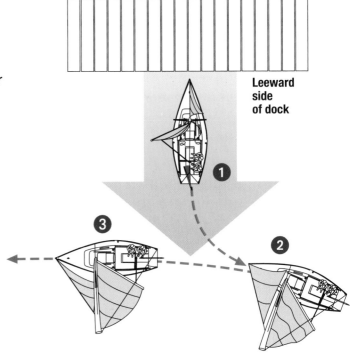

Leeward side of dock

Windward Side Departure

Windward side departures should be avoided. If at all possible, you should move your boat to the leeward side of the dock. If you ever have to make a windward departure, here's how to do it:

❶ With sails lowered, but ready to raise, move your boat to the end of the dock.

❷ At the end of the dock, raise the jib and push the boat away from the dock. Once clear of the dock, sheet in the jib to get the boat moving.

❸ When the boat has picked up enough speed, turn the boat into the wind and hoist the mainsail. Once the mainsail is up, turn to your course.

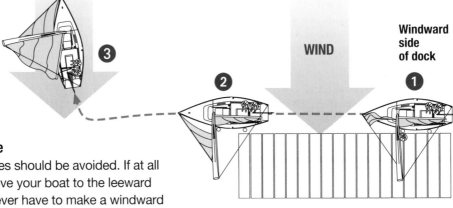

WIND

Windward side of dock

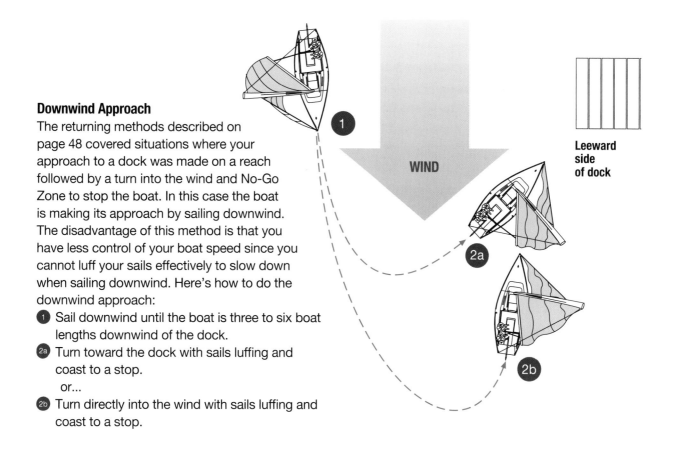

Downwind Approach

The returning methods described on page 48 covered situations where your approach to a dock was made on a reach followed by a turn into the wind and No-Go Zone to stop the boat. In this case the boat is making its approach by sailing downwind. The disadvantage of this method is that you have less control of your boat speed since you cannot luff your sails effectively to slow down when sailing downwind. Here's how to do the downwind approach:

1 Sail downwind until the boat is three to six boat lengths downwind of the dock.

2a Turn toward the dock with sails luffing and coast to a stop.

or...

2b Turn directly into the wind with sails luffing and coast to a stop.

Windward Side Approach

There may be times when you have no choice but to return to the windward side of the dock. The key point is to lower the mainsail when the boat is to windward of the dock and then drift down to it either with the jib up or lowered. Whether to leave the jib up depends on the conditions and the boat. If it's windy, it is usually a good idea to drop the jib so you won't drift downwind too quickly. It is very important that everyone is thoroughly briefed and understands what they should do and when, because timing is key to the success of a windward side approach. Make sure the fenders are in place before lowering the mainsail.

1 About 4-5 boat lengths upwind of your landing spot turn into the wind and drop your mainsail. Stow it so it won't get in the way.

2 Turn downwind toward the dock, using the jib to adjust your speed.

3 As you get near the dock let the jib luff completely or lower it. A crew member should be positioned with bow line in hand to step off on the dock and help slow the boat if necessary by taking a turn around a dock cleat.

PART 4

KNOTS AND LINES

A good knot is one that is secure with good holding power. It should also come untied easily so the line can be used. There are many knots used in sailing, but six basic, easy-to-tie knots will handle most, if not all, of your needs. Learn the knots well because an improperly tied knot is useless or worse.

The Bowline

The bowline (BOE-lin) puts a non-slipping loop at the end of a line. The knot becomes more secure under pressure, but remains easy to untie. It is a commonly used knot on sailboats. Among its many applications, the bowline is used to attach the jib sheets to the clew of the jib.

Laid line (top) consists of three large strands twisted around one another. Usually made of nylon, it is very strong but can be rough on the hands. Laid line stretches, which makes it excellent for anchor rode and docklines. Flexible braided line (bottom) made of Dacron™ is excellent for halyards and sheets. Dacron does not stretch as much as nylon, and braided line is relatively gentle on the hands. In addition to above lines, there is an ever changing assortment of new materials and construction methods designed for specific, higher tech applications. Low-stretch and low weight line can be great additions on board to increase sailing performance.

1 To tie a bowline, put a small loop in the line where you want the knot to be. Make sure the end crosses on top of the standing part of the line. This small loop will end up as part of the knot.

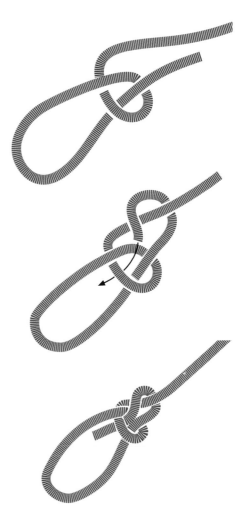

2 Run the end up through the loop you just made, down behind the standing part, back up over the edge of the loop, and down through the loop again.

3 Snug the knot together, making sure the knot holds and the remaining loop does not slip.

Figure-8 Knot

The figure-8 knot looks like its name. It is sometimes called a stopper knot, and is tied on the end of a line to keep the line from slipping through a fitting. Easy to untie, it is commonly used on the ends of the jib sheets in the cockpit.

❶ Pass the end over the standing part.

❷ Cross the end back under the standing part.

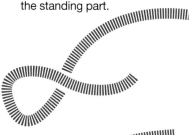

❸ Bring the end down through the loop. Tighten the knot.

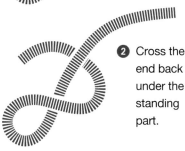

Square Knot

The square knot is used only for sail lashings. It is not recommended for tying two lines together because it can be difficult to untie. It is a good knot for a sail tie.

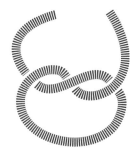

❶ Tie a simple overhand knot with the right end going over the left.

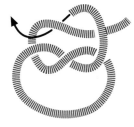

❷ Tie another simple overhand knot, this time crossing left end over right end.

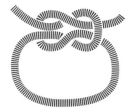

❸ As you tighten the line the knot should be symmetrical.

Sheet Bend

A sheet bend is used to tie two different sized lines together. It looks like a bowline, and it is secure and easy to untie.

❶ Make a loop at the end of the smaller line, with the end crossing over on top. Run the larger line up through the loop.

❷ Run the larger line down around the standing part of the smaller line, up over the edge of the loop, and down through the loop again.

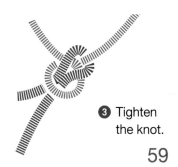

❸ Tighten the knot.

59

Clove Hitch

A clove hitch is used to tie a line to an object. It is not a very secure knot. It is very easily untied and, with an extra half-hitch, can be used to secure a tiller.

❶ Wrap a loop of the end around the object.

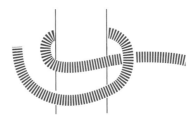

❷ Cross over the standing part and wrap a second loop around the object.

❸ Tuck the end under the crossing you just made and tighten.

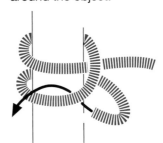

Round Turn and Two Half-hitches

This knot uses a loop to secure a line to an object.

❶ Wrap the end of the line twice around the object.

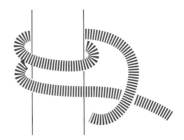

❷ Cross the end over the outside of the standing part.

❸ Use the end to tie two half-hitches onto the standing part.

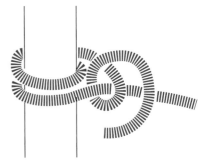

Simply cutting through a line will cause the cut ends to fray. A line should be treated with an electric hot knife to cut and fuse the ends. Whipping a line by wrapping the end of it with thread will protect it from fraying and unraveling. It's best to whip the line before cutting it.

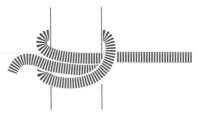

LINE HANDLING

A line should not be simply left in a tangled pile, but should always be ready to use or release by leaving it coiled.

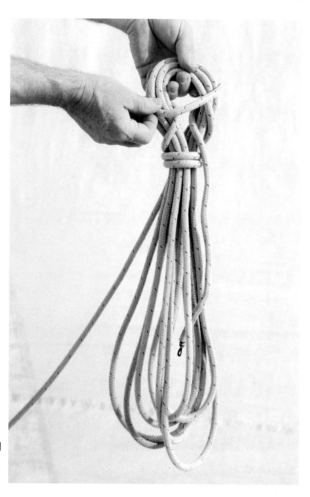

When coiling a line, one hand makes a new loop which is fed onto the other hand holding the loops previously coiled. With laid line it helps to twist the line slightly as you coil to avoid kinks or twists in the line. Twisting braided line may cause kinks and twists.

To stow a coiled line, wrap the end of the line around the middle of the coil. Make a loop and pass it through and over the upper end of the coil.

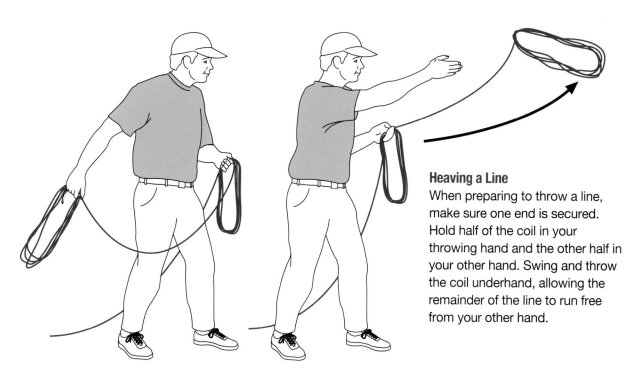

Heaving a Line
When preparing to throw a line, make sure one end is secured. Hold half of the coil in your throwing hand and the other half in your other hand. Swing and throw the coil underhand, allowing the remainder of the line to run free from your other hand.

WEATHER BASICS

Newspapers, radio, television, telephone, internet, and VHF radio forecasts keep sailors informed about predicted wind speed and direction, and storm possibilities.

Weather Maps help you predict what kind of weather to expect on the water. High pressure systems (Ⓗ) usually indicate good, mild weather, while low pressure systems (Ⓛ) usually are accompanied by a warm or cold front and inclement weather.

VHF Forecasts The National Oceanographic and Atmospheric Administration operates 400 VHF transmitters in the U.S. Each has a range of 40 miles and broadcasts short term weather forecasts. Seven frequencies are used for overlapping coverage. Ask your instructor which frequency is best for your area.

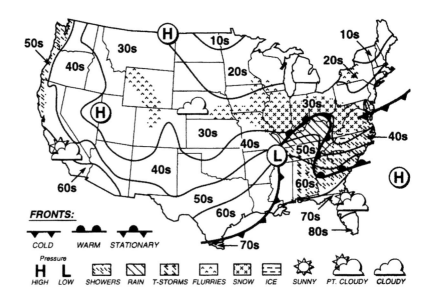

FRONTS:
COLD WARM STATIONARY

Pressure
H L
HIGH LOW SHOWERS RAIN T-STORMS FLURRIES SNOW ICE SUNNY PT. CLOUDY CLOUDY

Cumulus clouds, which are large, white, and fluffy, are often an indicator of good weather.

Wispy, thin **cirrus clouds** usually mean good weather for the day, but may be a prediction that a change in weather is on the way.

Towering **cumulonimbus clouds**, or "thunderheads" are usually accompanied by severe conditions, including heavy rain and lightning.

Low layered **stratus clouds** usually bring steady rain.

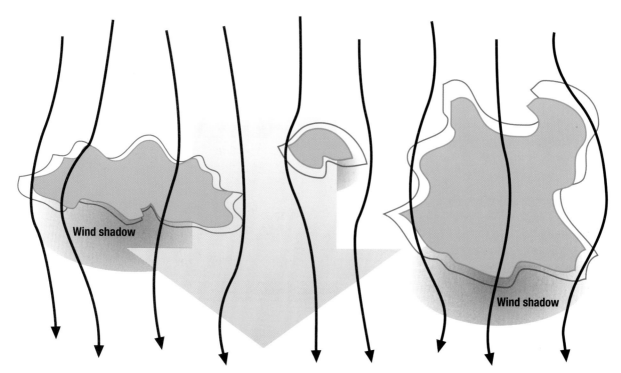

Land Effects

Wind conditions can be affected by nearby land features. Islands, tall buildings, even anchored ships cast *wind shadows* (areas of less wind) on their leeward sides. Sailing from fresh winds into one of these wind shadows greatly depowers a sailboat.

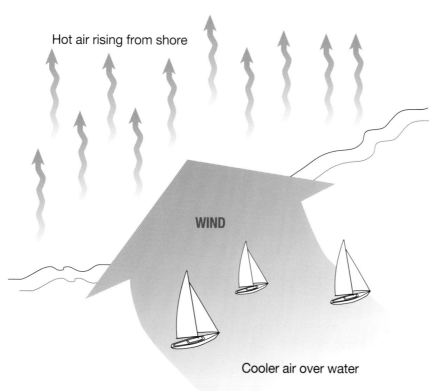

Hot air rising from shore

WIND

Cooler air over water

Thermal Winds

Local winds are often caused by differences in temperature between the shore and neighboring water. As denser cool air is drawn toward rising warm air, wind is created. These winds are commonly referred to as "onshore breezes" and "sea breezes." The technical term is *thermal wind*. The most famous illustration of thermal wind is on San Francisco Bay, where hot air rising out of the Sacramento Valley, about 75 miles inland from San Francisco, creates a vacuum that draws in 25-knot winds through the Golden Gate almost every summer afternoon like clockwork.

TIDES AND CURRENTS

Tides are the *vertical* change of water level and are caused primarily by the gravitational pull of the moon on the earth. As the moon rotates around the earth, it "pulls" the earth's water toward it. As the moon moves, so does the water level in most bodies of ocean water. Typically there are two high and two low tides each day on the East and West Coasts of the U.S. In the Gulf of Mexico there is usually only one high and one low per day. With a watch, a tide table and a chart you can determine the depth of the water in which you are sailing or anchoring at any given time.

Currents are the *horizontal* movement of water and are caused by river flow, wind, or ocean movements. The Gulf Stream off the East Coast of the U.S. is a well known ocean current. In coastal areas, currents are also caused by the tides rising and falling. Depending on their direction, these currents can either assist or hinder your progress while sailing. It is important to know the direction and strength of currents. Charts, tide tables, and a watch are helpful in planning your sail.

These photos, taken at the same location, show the difference between high and low tide. Consulting a tide table and a chart will help you avoid running aground during a low tide.

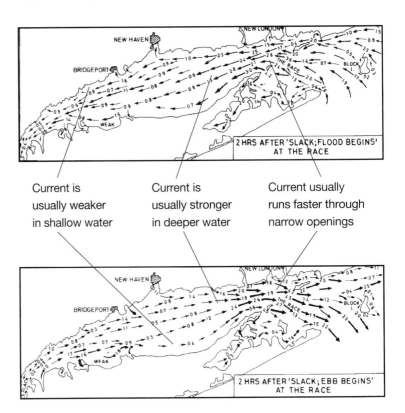

Current is usually weaker in shallow water

Current is usually stronger in deeper water

Current usually runs faster through narrow openings

While the photos above demonstrate *tide*, these charts from a nautical almanac show *current* coming in (*flooding*) and going out (*ebbing*) of Long Island Sound. Charts courtesy Reeds Nautical Almanac

Reading Tides and Current

There are a number of indicators on the water and shoreline that will tell you what the tide and currents are doing.

Current pulls on this buoy, causing it to lean, and leaves a wake as it flows from left to right.

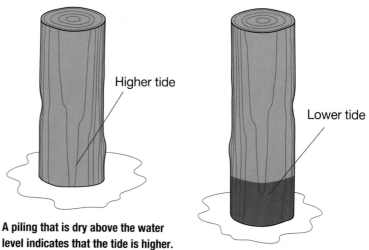

Higher tide

Lower tide

A piling that is dry above the water level indicates that the tide is higher. When the piling above the water is wet, the tide is lower. A beach can provide the same information as the piling. A dry beach is indicative of a higher tide level; a wet beach is a sign of a lower tide level.

Compensating for Current

If you are going to sail across a current you can compensate for the effect it will have on your boat. Instead of steering directly toward your goal, steer for a point upstream, and let the current pull you back to your desired course.

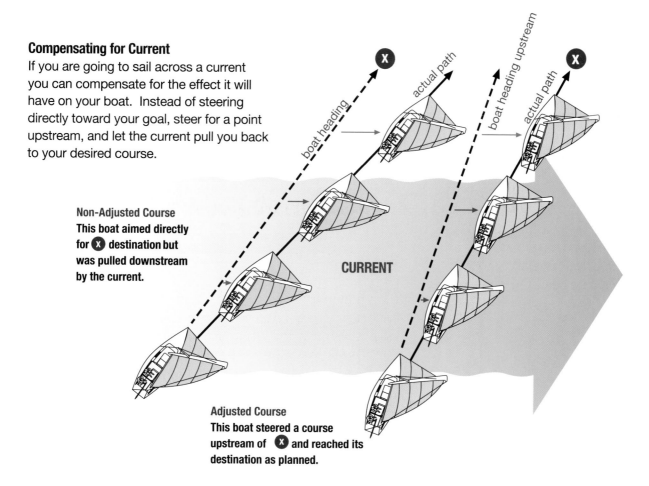

Non-Adjusted Course
This boat aimed directly for X destination but was pulled downstream by the current.

CURRENT

boat heading

actual path

boat heading upstream

actual path

Adjusted Course
This boat steered a course upstream of X and reached its destination as planned.

65

Basic Navigation Rules

The purpose of the Rules is to avoid collisions. The boat that is the *stand-on vessel* should maintain course and speed. The *give-way vessel* must keep out of the way and should make its change of course obvious and early. It is every vessel's obligation to avoid collisions, even if it is the stand-on vessel.

When sailing on **starboard tack**, the wind is coming over the *starboard* side of the boat. When sailing on **port tack**, the wind is coming over the *port* side of the boat.

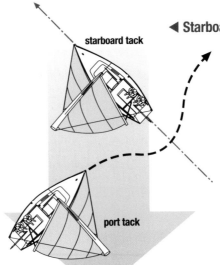

starboard tack

port tack

◀ Starboard Tack over Port Tack

A sailboat on a starboard tack has the right-of-way over a sailboat on a port tack. As boats on opposite tacks approach each other, the boat on the port tack is the *give-way vessel*. Its skipper should change course and aim well behind the stern of the starboard tack boat. The boat on starboard tack is the *stand-on vessel* and should hold its course.

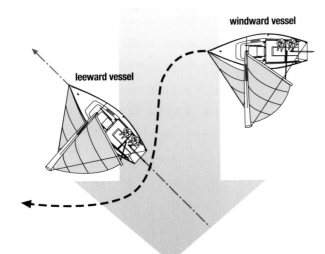

windward vessel

leeward vessel

◀ Leeward Vessel over Windward Vessel

When approaching another boat on the same tack the windward vessel, the boat upwind, is the *give-way vessel* and should yield to the leeward vessel by steering behind it. The leeward vessel is the *stand-on vessel* and should hold its course.

Overtaken Vessel over Overtaking Vessel ▶

A boat that is passing another should NOT expect the slower boat to clear a path. The boat that is doing the passing is the *give-way vessel*, and its skipper must change course to maneuver around the slower craft. The boat being overtaken is the *stand-on vessel* and should hold its course. A sailing vessel passing a powerboat must keep clear of the powerboat!

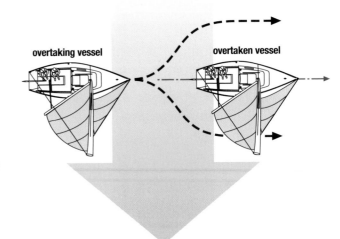

overtaking vessel

overtaken vessel

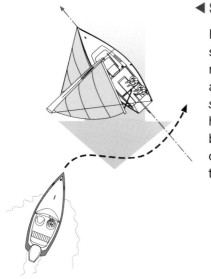

◀ Sailboats over Powerboats

Because a powerboat (or sailboat under power) is more maneuverable, it must yield to a sailboat. The sailboat is the *stand-on vessel* and should hold its course unless the other boat comes uncomfortably close. Then the sailboat should take evasive action.

Stay Clear of Large Vessels ▶

Ships and tugs with tows have difficulty in maneuvering. Always give them a wide berth, and you must give way when they are in a channel. If you see a tugboat crossing ahead, look well behind it to check if a barge is being towed. NEVER try to cross the cable between a tug and its tow.

In general, the priority for stand-on vessels, from top to bottom is:
1. A disabled vessel
2. A vessel that is difficult to maneuver, such as a dredge
3. A vessel restricted by draft, such as a tanker in a channel
4. A vessel engaged in commercial fishing
5. A sailboat
6. A powerboat

STAY ALERT. BE SAFE!

If you have any doubts about the other vessel's action, do not steer across its bow. If you are the *give-way vessel*, make your course change early and obvious to the other vessel.

BASIC NAVIGATION AIDS

Buoys and channel markers are like road signs and traffic markers on the water. While there are many kinds of buoys and channel markers in use in North America, the most common ones fall into the categories shown here. They have distinct shapes and colors that will help you sail your boat in and out of harbors safely and avoid shallow water. The basic rule to remember in U.S. waters is *"Red, Right, Returning."* This means keep the red markers to your right side when you are returning from open water into a harbor. Keep the green buoys on your right when leaving a harbor into open water.

Most buoys, channel markers and other navigation aids are marked on nautical charts. Local charts of your sailing area are available at most marine supply stores. It's a good idea to study a chart of your local area to get familiar with the "traffic signs" you will be encountering as you sail.

Green or red **lighted buoys** are spaced relatively far apart and located near the entrances of harbors. Each has a distinct flashing pattern that is indicated on a chart so it can be readily identified. Lighted buoys are especially helpful for navigating at night.

A **can** is an odd-numbered, green buoy that is used to mark the *left* side of a channel when entering (returning to) a harbor. It has a flat top. When you leave a harbor, cans mark the *right* side of the channel.

A **nun** is an even-numbered, red buoy used to mark the *right* side of a channel when entering (returning to) a harbor. It has a pointed top. When you leave a harbor, nuns mark the *left* side of the channel.

A **green daymark** is a square, odd-numbered green sign that is mounted to a piling. It marks the side of a channel and should be treated like a can.

A **red daymark** is a triangular, even-numbered, red sign mounted to a piling. It marks the right side of a channel when returning from sea.

READING A CHART

A chart shows not only the channels and the buoys, but also the shorelines, the water depth, obstructions, shoals, the positions of wrecks, and characteristics of the bottom. In addition, it indicates the positions of landmarks, lighthouses and much more. At the edge of the chart is an important note: "Soundings in Feet," "Soundings in Meters," or "Soundings in Fathoms" which tell you how the water depth is measured on the chart. A meter is a little over three feet, while a fathom is precisely six feet. Always check which measurement is used to indicate water depths (*soundings*) on your chart.

These diamond shapes are **channel buoys**. On a chart they are colored to represent a nun (red) or can (green). In this channel you can see a set of cans (on the left) and nuns (on the right) positioned to guide you safely through the narrow channel opening.

A **contour line** follows a constant water depth. On most charts, areas of shallower waters are indicated by a light blue area.

Charts also indicate **onshore landmarks** that can be used as navigation references. Here a tower is indicated.

Charts also indicate noteworthy bottom topography, such as hazardous rocks (shown), sunken ships and other **hidden dangers**.

The small numbers scattered throughout the water are **soundings** or depths at low tide at those particular points.

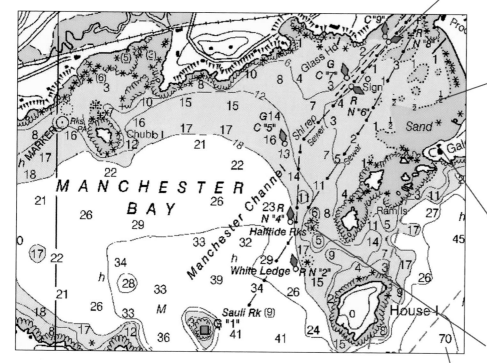

A **compass rose** (right) is printed on every nautical chart. If your boat has a compass, you use the compass rose to relate your boat's compass *heading* (direction) to a chart and vice versa. The outer circle indicates the degrees of the compass relative to the geographic north pole. The inner circle shows compass degrees relative to the magnetic north pole (yes, they're different). Your boat's compass relates to the inner circle (Magnetic North).

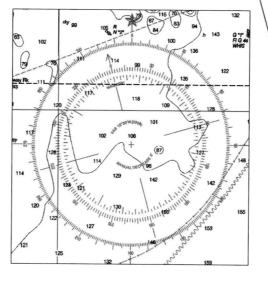

HYPOTHERMIA AND HEAT EMERGENCIES

Sailors are often exposed to extreme conditions. Hot, sunny days with no wind, cold rainy days with too much wind, prolonged exposure to wind and spray…all of the things that make sailing challenging and fun can sneak up on you if you do not take care of yourself. Your best preparation is to anticipate the extremes. Bring plenty of warm and waterproof clothing if it might get cool and wet. Drink plenty of fluids and wear a hat in hot, sunny weather. Hypothermia and heat emergencies can occur. Here are some signals and solutions.

HEAT EXHAUSTION

SIGNALS…
- Cool, moist, pale skin
- Heavy sweating
- Headache
- Dizziness
- Nausea
- Weakness, exhaustion

TREATMENT…
Without prompt care, heat exhaustion can advance to a more serious condition — heat stroke. First aid includes:
- Move person to cool environment
- Remove clothing soaked with perspiration and loosen any tight clothing
- Apply cool, wet towels or sheets
- Fan the person
- Give person a half glass (4 oz.) of cool water every 15 minutes

HEAT STROKE

SIGNALS…
- Red, hot, dry or moist skin
- Very high temperature
- Changes in level of consciousness
- Vomiting
- Rapid, weak pulse
- Rapid, shallow breathing

TREATMENT…
Heat stroke is life threatening. Anyone suffering from heat stroke needs to be cooled and an EMS technician should be contacted immediately. To care for heat stroke.
- Move person to cool environment
- Apply cool, wet towels or sheets.
- If available, place ice or cold pacs on the person's wrists and ankles, groin, each armpit, and neck
- If unconscious, check breathing and pulse

HYPOTHERMIA

SIGNALS…
- Shivering
- Impaired judgment
- Dizziness
- Numbness
- Change in level of consciousness
- Weakness
- Glassy stare
- Physical symptoms may vary, since age, body size, and clothing will cause individual differences.

TREATMENT…
Medical assistance should be given to anyone with hypothermia. Until medical assistance arrives,these steps should be taken:
- Check breathing and pulse.
- Move the person to a warm place.
- Remove all wet clothing. Gradually warm the person by wrapping in blankets or putting on dry clothes. Do not warm a person too quickly, such as immersing in warm water. Rapid rewarming may cause dangerous heart rhythms. Hot water bottles and chemical heat packs may be used if first wrapped in a towel or blanket before applying.
- Give warm, nonalcoholic and non-caffeinated liquids to a conscious person only.

The accompanying immersion survival chart (below) shows that any water temperature can kill depending on the duration of the immersion. The table (below right) depicts some examples of time periods that a person may be able to survive in various water temperatures. (Adapted from U.S. Coast Guard Auxiliary 8th District)

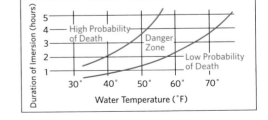

Water Temp.	Wearing Life Jacket	Treading Water	Swimming
70 degrees	18 hours	13 hours	10 hours
55 degrees	3.5 hours	3 hours	2 hours
35 degrees	1.75 hours	1.25 hours	1.75 hours

ELECTRICAL HAZARDS

While there are hazards on the water and on your boat, there's one very important hazard you need to look up to see. *Electrical powerlines can be deadly!* Make sure you have the proper clearance before crossing under powerlines, especially when moving boats on trailers onshore. Remember to take into account higher water levels from tides, river runoff, or recent rains.

Another electrical danger in some regions is lightning. Should you be overtaken during a lightning storm, you should head immediately for port and keep your crew away from the mast and any metal or electrical components aboard your boat.

PRE-SAILING EXERCISES

Before any exercise, including sailing, you should warm up and loosen up by stretching. Keep yourself in reasonably good condition, and before heading out, stretch out. These flexibility exercises should be done for about 30 seconds. Do not stretch to the point of pain, only to increase flexibility.

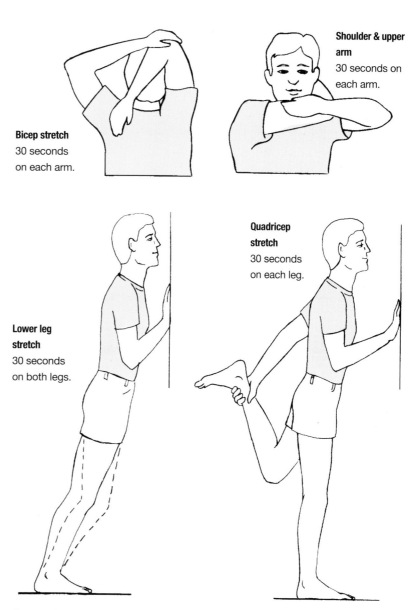

Bicep stretch
30 seconds on each arm.

Shoulder & upper arm
30 seconds on each arm.

Lower leg stretch
30 seconds on both legs.

Quadricep stretch
30 seconds on each leg.

Sailing requires movements in many unusual positions. Stretching before and after you sail will help minimize the stiffness and discomfort that commonly accompanies using new muscle groups. *NOTE: Do not engage in any of these exercises without consulting with your physician. Some of these exercises could adversely affect students who are not physically fit or have a history of back, shoulder or knee problems.*

OVERBOARD RESCUE

All sailors must know how to react quickly to a crew overboard situation. There are two preferred methods of rescuing a crew who has fallen overboard. All involve the following seven steps:

1. *Get buoyancy to the Person in water (PIW).*
2. *Keep the PIW in sight.*
3. *Head the boat back to the PIW.*
4. *Stop the boat alongside the PIW.*
5. *Make contact with the PIW.*
6. *Attach the PIW to the boat.*
7. *Get the PIW back on board.*

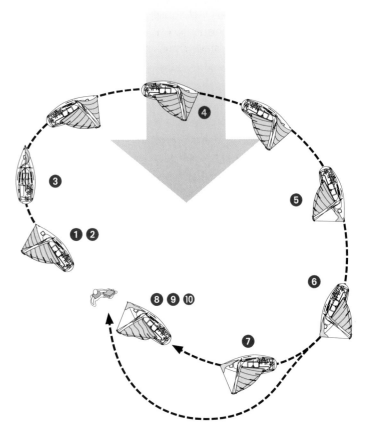

Quick-Stop Rescue

The hallmark of the Quick-Stop Rescue method is the immediate reduction of boat speed by turning in a direction to windward and thereafter maneuvering at modest speed, remaining near the PIW. This rescue requires these steps:

❶ As soon as a crew member falls overboard, throw buoyant objects, such as cushions, life jackets or life rings, to the PIW and shout *"Crew Overboard!"* These objects may not only come to the aid of the PIW, but will "litter the water" where he or she went overboard and help the spotter to keep him or her in view. It has been determined that the deployment of the standard overboard pole rig requires too much time. The pole rig is saved to "put on top" of the person in case the initial maneuver is unsuccessful.

❷ Designate someone to spot and point at the PIW. The spotter should NEVER take his or her eyes off the PIW.

❸ Bring the boat into the wind, trimming the mainsail and jib to close-hauled.

❹ Continue to turn through the wind, without releasing the headsail, until the wind is almost astern. Do not ease the sails.

❺ Hold this course until the PIW is aft of the beam, and drop or furl the headsail if possible. If the headsail is lowered, its sheets should not be slacked.

❻ Jibe the boat.

❼ Steer toward the PIW as if you were going to pick up a mooring.

❽ Stop the boat alongside the PIW by easing or backing sails.

❾ Establish contact with the PIW with a heaving line or other device. A "throwing sock" containing 75 feet of light floating line and a kapok bag can be thrown into the wind because the line is kept inside the bag and trails out as it sails to the PIW. Attach the PIW to the boat.

❿ Bring the PIW on board.

This method should be executed under sail alone unless there is insufficient wind to maneuver the boat.

Figure-8 Rescue

Figure-8 rescue avoids jibing during a rescue. In heavy weather, you may find controlling the boat easier with this rescue technique; *however, it is imperative to keep the PIW in sight at all times!* Take the following steps in a Figure-8 rescue:

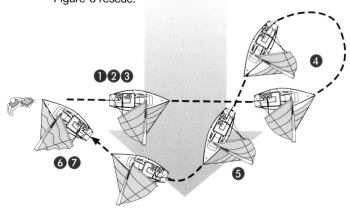

1. As soon as a crew member falls overboard, call out LOUDLY *"Crew overboard!"*

2. Throw cushions, life jackets or life rings in the direction of the PIW. Steer the boat on a beam reach.

3. Assign a crew member to watch and point at the PIW. This crew member should NEVER take his or her eyes off the PIW.

4. After sailing a maximum of four boatlengths, tack and fall off onto a deep broad reach, crossing the boat's original course.

5. The plan is to approach the PIW on a close reach. This point of sail gives perfect speed control, using the main sheet as a "gas pedal," together with some space for altering direction. To determine whether you're in position for the close-reach approach, steer toward the PIW and let off your sheets. If you are on a close reach, both sails will flog. If your approach is too far upwind, your main will fill and slowing down will be impossible. In this case immediately run off almost dead downwind for a length or two. Then steer up for the PIW again. In all probability this will position you properly for a close-reach approach. Should you still be too far upwind with a mainsail full of air, bear off hard a second time, etc.

6. Ease sheets to slow the boat and bring it to a stop alongside the PIW.

7. Attach the PIW to the boat and bring on board.

Attachment. After maneuvering the boat back alongside the PIW, it is imperative that the PIW be attached to the boat. This should be done so that the boat and PIW do not drift apart, necessitating another return. Do not rely on the PIW holding onto a line. In descending order of preference, here are some methods:

- Use a Lifesling, if you have one.
- Use the "D" rings of an inflatable harness (if being worn) to tie the PIW to the boat.
- Tie a bowline around the PIW.
- Once the PIW is attached, drop the sails. Do not leave the PIW tied to the boat unattended.

Retrieval. This is considerably easier if there are more than two crew members left aboard to assist. On a boat with low freeboard, the crew can often drag the PIW aboard. In flat water, and if the boat has a scoop/swim platform, the PIW can be dragged up over the stern. If shorthanded, you may need to improvise some method to aid in the retrieval:

- A line over the side with a bowline tied in the end to act as a stirrup. Any lines over the side should be tied onto the boat on the opposite side from the PIW so they can help themselves get onboard.
- A line over the side with a series of loops tied at intervals so the PIW can assist themselves, or even climb back in unassisted.
- A paddle over the side tied in the middle so it becomes a "T" bar for the PIW to stand on.
- A block and tackle (preferably four parts) rigged to a pre-hoisted halyard that is then used to lift the PIW from the water.

If you are unable to retrieve the PIW, ensure that the PIW is securely attached to the boat, and call for help on the VHF radio (MAYDAY), or attract the help of a passing boat.

Aftercare. Be aware that the PIW may be suffering from hypothermia (see page 70). Get the PIW back ashore as soon as possible. Unless you are sailing in tropical waters, you should treat this as a serious first aid issue.

SHORTENING SAIL

When the wind is too strong and your boat is heeling too much, you should shorten your sail. Your boat will go just as fast and will be more in control with less sail area exposed to the wind.

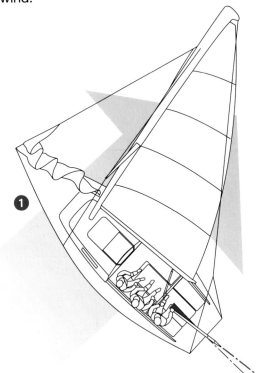

Reefing

The area of the mainsail may be reduced by lowering the sail partially and securing the lower portion to the boom. This is best accomplished while on a close reach or while Hove-To with the mainsail luffing.

Lowering the Jib

The easiest way to reduce sail is to simply lower the jib. With just the mainsail up, however, the boat is no longer in balance. The wind pressure on the mainsail will tend to rotate the bow of the boat toward the wind. To compensate, you will need to steer with the tiller pulled slightly away from the mainsail ❶ to keep the boat sailing straight. Not all boats will sail to windward with the jib down.

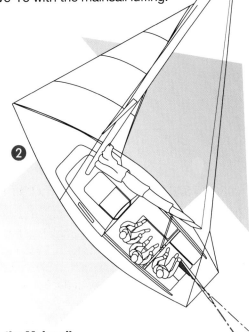

Lowering the Mainsail

The most significant way you can reduce sail is to lower the mainsail. With just the jib up, however, the boat is no longer in balance. The wind pressure on the jib will tend to rotate the bow of the boat away from the wind. To compensate, you will need to steer with the tiller pushed slightly toward the mainsail ❷ to keep the boat sailing straight.

RUNNING AGROUND

Running aground happens to almost every sailor at some time. If you run aground on a soft, muddy bottom with a rising tide, you'll float off easily with no damage to the boat.

If you get stuck, use the sails and crew weight to heel the boat. You may have to get some crew members to sit on the boom and slowly swing it out over the side to tilt the boat enough to raise the keel off the bottom.

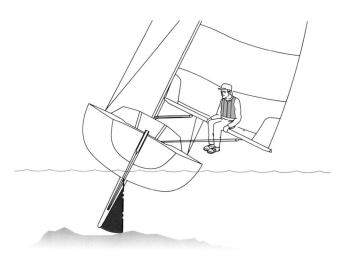

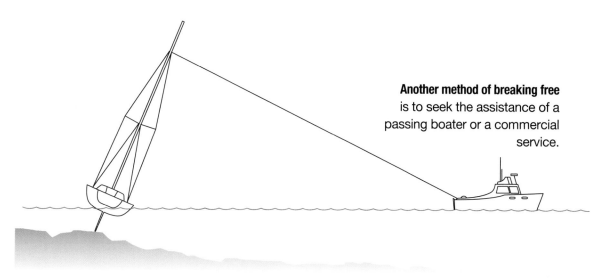

Another method of breaking free is to seek the assistance of a passing boater or a commercial service.

MORE ON SAILING EMERGENCY PROCEDURES

Knockdowns. A knockdown is when a boat heels over so far that one of its spreaders touches the water. This usually happens because it has been carrying too much sail for high wind conditions or because of a mistake by the helmsman or crew. To recover from a knockdown:

▶ Release the sheets and the boom vang.
▶ Get the crew up to the windward rail.
▶ If the rudder responds, head up until the sails luff.

Swamping. A knockdown may cause the boat to fill with water if hatches are left open. If your boat becomes swamped:

▶ Release the sheets.
▶ Lower the sails.
▶ Bail with buckets and bilge pump.

Sinking. If your boat is taking on water and is in danger of sinking:

▶ Make sure everyone is wearing a life jacket.
▶ Bail with buckets and bilge pump.
▶ If the boat has been holed, try to find the source of the leak and plug it.
▶ Try to sail to shore and run it aground before it goes down.
▶ If the boat becomes completely swamped with decks awash, and it looks like it will sink, DO NOT leave the boat...let it leave you by going down.
▶ Make sure you are not tangled in any lines.

ANCHORING

As in docking, preparation is the key to successful anchoring. Before anchoring take down and stow the jib. Make sure the foredeck is clear except for the anchor and its line (*rode*), which should be coiled on the deck (laid out in large loops) so it will run freely. If there is a pulpit, make sure the anchor and rode will run under it.

❶ When everything is prepared, sail **on a reach**, about 3-6 boat lengths downwind of where you want to drop your anchor. When you are directly downwind of where you want to drop it, head up into the wind.

❷ **As the boat comes to a stop**, lower (do not throw or drop) the anchor. After it hits the bottom pay out the anchor line as you drift back.

❸ **When you've reached the spot** where you want the boat to remain, firmly cleat off the rode. Check for adequate scope and that your anchor is holding. Then lower your mainsail.

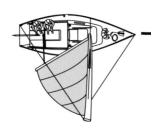

The Danforth anchor is very common. It is strong, lightweight, holds well, and is easy to store.

Scope

The amount of rode that you pay out is not arbitrary. Scope is the ratio of anchor rode to the depth of the water. Plus freeboard and allowing for tidal range. A scope of 7:1 is considered adequate for most conditions. This means that if the depth of the water where you are anchoring is 10 feet and your freeboard is 2 feet, and the tide will rise 3 feet, you should pay out 105 feet of rode. 10 + 2 + 3) x 7 = 105 Charts list the depth of the water at low tide, so check your tide table to determine the rise of the tide for the period you will be anchored.

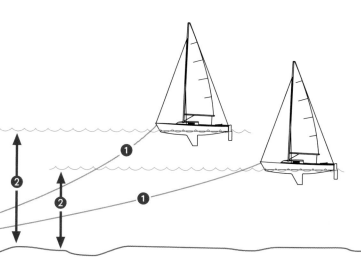

Scope is the ratio of the length of your anchor rode ❶ to the depth of the water ❷ plus freeboard and allowing for any tidal rise.

Is your anchor holding?

It's good seamanship to make sure your anchor has a secure hold on the bottom. Here's an easy method: Once you think you've anchored well, sight two objects that are aligned, for instance, a buoy and a house. Both objects can be on shore, such as a fence post and a telephone pole. Do NOT use another boat as one of your objects for sighting.

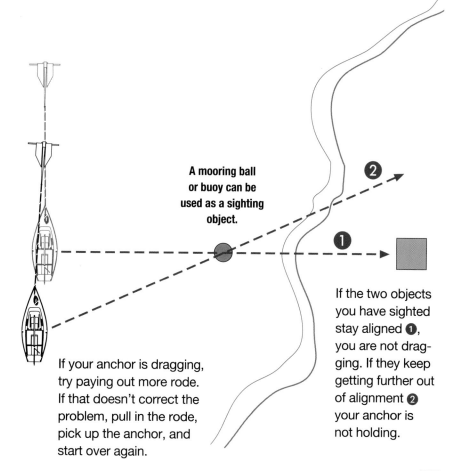

A mooring ball or buoy can be used as a sighting object.

If your anchor is dragging, try paying out more rode. If that doesn't correct the problem, pull in the rode, pick up the anchor, and start over again.

If the two objects you have sighted stay aligned ❶, you are not dragging. If they keep getting further out of alignment ❷ your anchor is not holding.

SAFETY EQUIPMENT

There are a number of safety requirements specified by the U.S. Coast Guard for sailors operating boats on lakes, rivers and the open ocean. Specific information can be gained from a pamphlet titled "Federal Requirements for Recreational Boats." A current copy can be obtained from most chandleries, U.S.C.G. stations or by writing U.S. Coast Guard, 2100 Second St. SW, Washington, DC 20593. We have provided a summary of current requirements.

The U.S. Coast Guard requires pleasure boats to carry safety equipment. This equipment list is a *minimum* and should be augmented by the boat owner.

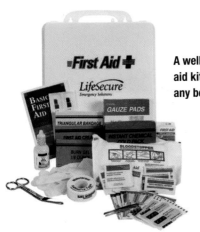

A well-equipped first aid kit is a necessity on any boat.

Safety Checklist
▶ Recreational boats are bound by both federal, state and municipal requirements.
▶ Your boat must be registered in the state of principal use and have a Certificate of Number. This number must be displayed per state requirements. Any change in ownership, address change or boat status must be registered with the state within 15 days.
▶ The U.S.C.G or any law enforcement officials may board your vessel when you are underway and terminate use of your vessel for negligent operation or violation of federal regulations.
▶ U.S.C.G. approved fire extinguishers must be carried aboard all auxiliary powered vessels. Boats less than 26 feet must have one Type B-1.
▶ U.S.C.G. approved life jackets, Type I, II, III or V are required for each person aboard the vessel and one Type IV (throwable) for vessels larger than 16 feet in length.
▶ U.S.C.G. approved Visual Distress Signals must be carried aboard vessels except: boats less than 16 feet in length, boats in organized events such as regattas, open sailboats less than 26 feet in length without auxiliary power, and manually propelled boats.
▶ All vessels must carry an efficient sound producing device.
▶ Vessels operating or anchored between sunset and sunrise are required to display navigation lights.
▶ Vessels with divers in the water must display a rigid replica of the code flag "A". In many states these vessels must display a red flag with a diagonal white stripe.
▶ U.S. law prohibits dumping of refuse in U.S. waters. This includes plastics, oil and hazardous waste.
▶ Vessels equipped with Marine Sanitation Devices must meet U.S.C.G. requirements.
▶ Boating accidents must be reported to the nearest state authority per the federal requirements.
▶ You are obligated to render assistance, as can be safely provided, to anyone in danger at sea.

Recommended Safety Equipment
▶ Additional means of propulsion such as oars, paddle or auxiliary power.
▶ A manual bailing device such as a bucket or bilge pump.
▶ A basic first aid kit with instructions.
▶ An anchor and anchor line.
▶ A tool kit, spare parts and through-hull plugs.
▶ A VHF radio.
▶ Navigation charts and magnetic compass.

SIGNALING FOR HELP

Before you decide to ask for outside assistance, determine if you can take care of the problem yourself. You may be able to get back to the harbor under your own power, or accept a tow from a friendly boat. U.S. Coast Guard and private search-and-rescue missions are expensive and time-consuming. If you do need to signal for help, use the signals, either separately or together, that are recognized by the U.S. Coast Guard and the Navigation Rules.

International Distress Signals

- ▶ A smoke signal giving off orange-colored smoke.
- ▶ A rocket parachute flare or a hand flare showing a red light.
- ▶ Rockets or shells, throwing red stars fired one at a time at short intervals.
- ▶ Flashlight or other device signaling SOS (*dot-dot-dot, dash-dash-dash, dot-dot-dot*) in the Morse Code.
- ▶ Continuous sounding of a foghorn.
- ▶ Flames, such as a fire in a bucket or barrel.
- ▶ "Mayday" spoken over a VHF Radio.
- ▶ A signal consisting of a square flag having above or below it a ball or anything resembling a ball.
- ▶ Flying the international code flags or signals "N" and "C".
- ▶ Firing a gun or other explosive device at intervals of about a minute.
- ▶ Slowly and repeatedly waving both outstretched arms.
- ▶ A high intensity white light flashing at regular intervals from 50 to 70 times per minute.
- ▶ A radiotelegraph or radiotelephone alarm signal.
- ▶ Signals transmitted by an Emergency Position-Indicating Radio Beacon (EPIRB).

USE AND REGULATIONS FOR FLARES:
Flares fired from a pistol or launcher are visible over the horizon day or night. Handheld flares can pinpoint your location for rescuers, but should be held downwind and used with great caution. The U.S. Coast Guard requires vessels over 16 feet to have three daylight and three night flares or three combination daylight/night devices readily available, which have not expired.

Rig Types

The **cutter** is a sloop with its mast near the middle of the hull, allowing space to fly a second jib.

The **yawl** has two masts. Its mizzen (smaller) mast is behind the rudder post.

The **ketch** is another two masted boat. The mizzen (smaller) mast is in front of the rudder post.

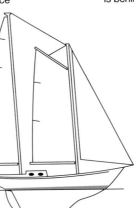

The **schooner** has two or more masts, with the tallest usually in back.

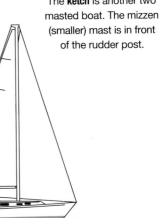

The marconi-rigged **sloop** is the most common modern rig. It's excellent for sailing upwind.

A cat rig has no jib. This two-masted example is also a ketch rig. Hence the name **cat ketch**.

Most modern **multihulls** are sloop-rigged. Their mainsails have full-length battens and a large curved roach (leech).

The traditional **gaff rig** has a four-sided mainsail with a wooden spar (gaff) attached to the top.

Hull Types

A monohull is a boat with a single hull.

The twin-hulled catamaran features speed and acceleration.

The three-hulled trimaran can also carry a lot of sail for speed.

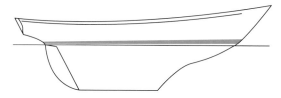

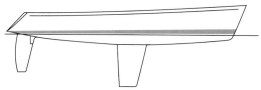

The traditional **full keel** allows for a deep interior and excellent straight-line tracking.

The **fin keel and spade rudder** reduces drag and improves maneuverability.

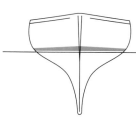

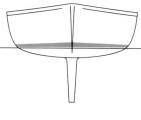

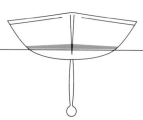

A deep **"wineglass" hull** provides gentle motion and ample interior volume.

A shallow hull with a **fin keel** is a great performer, especially downwind.

A **winged-keel** allows a shallow keel to perform more efficiently.

A **bulb keel** concentrates weight at its bottom, improving stability.

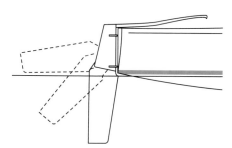

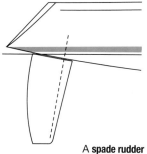

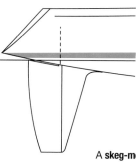

Some small keelboats have retractable **outboard rudders** which allow them to travel in shallow waters and swing back on impact.

A **spade rudder** is efficient but unprotected from impact.

A **skeg-mounted rudder** is strong and well protected.

81

Glossary

A

Abeam - off the side of (at right angle to) the boat.

Aboard - on the boat.

Adrift - a boat drifting without control.

Aft - at or toward the stern or behind the boat.

Aground - a boat whose keel is touching the bottom.

Amidships - toward the center of the boat.

Apparent wind - the wind aboard a moving boat.

Astern - behind the stern of the boat.

Athwartships - across the boat from side to side.

B

Backstay - the standing rigging running from the stern to the top of the mast, keeping the mast from falling forward.

Back - to stop or to propel a boat backward by holding the clew of a sail out to windward.

Bail - to empty a boat of water.

Balance - the capability of a boat to sail straight without changing the tiller position.

Ballast - weight in the keel of a boat that provides stability.

Barometer - a weather forecasting instrument that measures air pressure.

Batten - a thin slat that slides into a pocket in the leech of a sail, helping it hold its shape.

Beam - the width of a boat at its widest point.

Beam reach - (point of sail) sailing in a direction at approximately 90 degrees to the wind.

Bear away - to fall off, head away from the wind.

Bearing - the direction from one object to another expressed in compass degrees.

Beating - a course sailed upwind.

Below - the area of a boat beneath the deck.

Bend - to attach a sail to a spar or a headstay, or to attach a line to a sail.

Bight - a loop in a line.

Bilge - the lowest part of the boat's interior, where water on board will collect.

Bitter end - the end of a line.

Blanket - to use a sail or object to block the wind from filling a sail.

Block - a pulley on a boat.

Boat hook - a pole with a hook on the end used for grabbing hold of a mooring or retrieving something that has fallen overboard.

Boat speed - the speed of a boat through the water.

Bolt rope - the rope sewn into the foot and luff of some mainsails and the luff of some jibs by which the sails are attached to the boat.

Boom - the spar extending directly aft from the mast to which the foot of the mainsail is attached.

Boom vang - a block and tackle system which pulls the boom down to assist sail control.

Bottom - 1. - the underside of the boat.
2. - the land under the water.

Bow - the forward part of the boat.

Bow line (BOW - line) - a line running from the bow of the boat to the dock or mooring.

Bowline - (BOE-lin) - a knot designed to make a loop that will not slip and can be easily untied.

Breast line - a short dockline leading off the beam of the boat directly to the dock.

Broach - an uncontrolled rounding up into the wind, usually from a downwind point of sail.

Broad reach - (point of sail) sailing in a direction with the wind at the rear corner of the boat (approximately 135 degrees from the bow).

Bulkhead - a wall that runs athwartships on a boat, usually providing structural support to the hull.

Buoy - a floating marker.

Buoyancy - the ability of an object to float.

By the lee - sailing on a run with the wind coming over the same side of the boat as the boom.

C

Cabin - the interior of a boat.

Can - an odd-numbered, green, flat-topped buoy marking the left side of a channel as you return to port.

Capsize - to tip or turn a boat over.

Cast off - to release a line when leaving a dock or mooring.

Catamaran - a twin-hulled sailing vessel with a deck or trampoline between the hulls.

Catboat - a boat with only a mainsail and the mast located at the bow.

Centerboard - a pivoting board that can be lowered and used like a keel to keep a boat from slipping to leeward.

Centerline - the midline of a boat running from bow to stern.

Chafe - wear on a line caused by rubbing.

Chainplates - strong metal plates which connect the shrouds to the boat.

Channel - a (usually narrow) path in the water, marked by buoys, in which the water is deep enough to sail.

Chart - a nautical map.

Charter - to rent a boat.

Chock - a guide mounted on the deck through which docklines and anchor rode are run.

Chop - rough, short, steep waves.

Cleat - a nautical fitting that is used to secure a line.

Clew - the lower, aft corner of a sail. The clew of the mainsail is held taut by the outhaul. The jib sheets are attached to the clew of the jib.

Close-hauled - the point of sail that is closest to the wind.

Close reach - (point of sail) sailing in a direction with the wind forward of the beam (about 70 degrees from the bow).

Coaming - the short protective wall surrounding the cockpit.

Cockpit - the lower area in which the steering controls and sail controls are located.

Coil - to loop a line neatly so it can be stored.

Come about - see **tack**.

Companionway - the steps leading from the cockpit or deck to the cabin below.

Compass - the magnetic instrument which indicates the direction in which the boat is headed.

Compass rose - the twin circles on a chart which indicate the direction of true north and magnetic north.

Course - the direction in which the boat is steered.

Crew - besides the skipper, anyone on board who helps sail the boat.

Cunningham - a line running through a grommet about eight inches up from the tack of a mainsail that is used to tighten the luff of the sail.

Current - the horizontal movement of water caused by tides, wind and other forces.

Cutter - a single-masted boat with the mast near the middle that is capable of flying both a jib and a staysail.

D

Daysailer - a small sailboat.

Dead downwind - sailing in a direction straight downwind.

Deck - the mostly flat surface area on top of the boat.

Depower - to release the power from the sails by allowing them to luff or making them flatter. This is done to reduce heel.

Dinghy - a small sailboat or rowboat.

Displacement - the weight of a boat; therefore the amount of water it displaces.

Dock - 1. - the wooden structure where a boat may be tied up.

2. - the act of bringing the boat to rest alongside the structure.

Dockline - a line used to secure the boat to the dock.

Dodger - a canvas protection in front of the cockpit of some boats that is designed to keep spray off the skipper and crew.

Downhaul - a line used to pull down on the movable gooseneck on some boats to tighten the luff of the mainsail. The Cunningham has the same function on other boats.

Downwind - away from the direction of the wind.

Draft - the depth of a boat's keel from the water's surface.

E

Ease - to let out a line or sail.

Ebb - an outgoing current.

F

Fairlead - a fitting that guides a jib sheet or other lines back to the cockpit or along the deck.

Fairway - a channel.

Fake - to lay out a line on deck using large loops to keep it from becoming tangled.

Fall off - see **Head down**.

Fast - secured.

Fathom - a measurement of the depth of water. One fathom equals six feet.

Fender - a rubber bumper used to protect a boat by keeping it from hitting a dock.

Fend off - push off.

Fetch - a course on which a boat can make its destination without having to tack.

Fitting - a piece of nautical hardware.

Figure-8 knot - a knot designed to act as a stopper in the end of a line that takes the form of an eight.

Figure-8 rescue - a manuever used to return to a person or object in the water.

Flood - an incoming current.

Flooding - a vessel taking on water.

Following sea - waves hitting the boat from astern.

Foot - the bottom edge of a sail.

Fore - forward.

Forepeak - a storage area in the bow (below the deck).

Foresail - a jib or a genoa.

Forestay - the standing rigging running from the bow to the mast to which, the jib is hanked on.

Forward - toward the bow.

Fouled - tangled.

Foul-weather gear - water-resistant clothing.

Freeboard - the height of the hull above the water's surface.

Full - not luffing.

Furl - to fold or roll up a sail.

G

Gaff - on some boats, a spar along the top edge of a four-sided sail.

Gear - generic term for sailing equipment.

GLOSSARY

Genoa - a large jib whose clew extends aft of the mast.

Give-way vessel - the vessel required to give way to another boat when they may be on a collision course.

Glide zone - the distance a sailboat takes to coast to a stop.

Gooseneck - the strong fitting that connects the boom to the mast.

Grommet - a reinforcing metal ring set in a sail.

Ground tackle - the anchor and rode (chain and line).

Gudgeon - a fitting attached to the stern of a boat into which the pintles of a rudder are inserted.

Gunwale (GUN-el) - the edge of the deck where it meets the topsides.

Gust - see **puff**.

H

Halyard - a line used to hoist or lower a sail.

Hank - a snap hook that is used to connect the luff of a jib onto the forestay.

"Hard a-lee" - the command given to the crew just prior to tacking.

Hard over - to turn the tiller as far as possible in one direction.

Hatch - a large covered opening in the deck.

Haul in - to tighten a line.

Head - 1. - the top corner of a sail. 2. - the bathroom on a boat. 3. - the toilet on a boat.

Headboard - the reinforcing small board affixed to the head of a sail.

Header - a wind shift which makes your boat head down or sails to be sheeted in.

Heading - the direction of the boat expressed in compass degrees.

Head down - to fall off or bear away, changing course away from the wind.

Head off - see **head down**.

Head up - to come up, changing course toward the wind.

Headsail - a jib, genoa, or staysail.

Headstay - the standing rigging running from the bow to the mast.

Head-to-wind - the course of the boat when the bow is dead into the wind.

Headway - progress made forward.

Heave - to throw.

Heave-to - to hold one's position in the water by using the force of the sails and rudder to counter one another.

Heavy weather - strong winds and large waves.

Heel - the lean of a boat caused by the wind.

Helm - the tiller.

Helmsman - the person responsible for steering the boat.

High side - the windward side of the boat.

Hike - to position crew members out over the windward rail to help balance the boat.

Hiking stick - see **tiller extension**.

Hiking strap - a strap used by people hiking out that holds their feet.

Holding ground - the bottom ground in an anchorage used to hold the anchor.

Hove-to - a boat that has completed the process of heaving-to, with its jib aback, its main loosely trimmed, and its rudder securely positioned to steer it close to the wind.

Hull - the body of the boat, excluding rig and sails.

Hull speed - the theoretical maximum speed of a sailboat determined by the length of its waterline.

I

Inboard - inside of the rail of a boat.

In irons - a boat that is head-to-wind, making no forward headway.

J

Jib - the small forward sail of a boat attached to the forestay.

Jibe - to change direction of a boat by steering the stern through the wind.

"Jibe-ho" - the command given to the crew when starting a jibe.

Jiffy reef - a quick reefing system allowing a section of the mainsail to be tied to the boom.

Jury rig - an improvised, temporary repair.

K

Kedge off - to use an anchor to pull a boat into deeper water after it has run aground.

Keel - the heavy vertical fin beneath a boat that helps keep it upright and prevents it from slipping sideways in the water.

Ketch - a two-masted boat with its mizzen (after) mast shorter than its mainmast and located forward of the rudder post.

Knockdown - a boat heeled so far that one of its spreaders touches the water.

Knot - one nautical mile per hour.

L

Land breeze - a wind that blows over land and out to sea.

Lash - to tie down.

Lay - to sail a course that will clear an obstacle without tacking.

Lazarette - a storage compartment built into the cockpit or deck.

Lazy sheet - the windward side jib sheet that is not under strain.

Lead (LEED) - to pass a line through a fitting or a block.

Lee helm - the boat's tendency to turn away from the wind.

Lee shore - land which is on the leeward side of the boat. Because the wind is blowing in that direction, a lee shore could pose a danger.

Leech - the after edge of a sail.

Leeward (LEW-erd) - the direction away from the wind (where the wind is blowing to).

Leeward side - the side of the boat or sail that is away from the wind.

Leeway - sideways slippage of the boat in a direction away from the wind.

Lifeline - wire supported by stanchions, around the outside of the deck to help prevent crew members from falling overboard.

Life Jacket - is piece of equipment designed to assist a wearer, who may be either conscious or unconscious, to keep afloat.

Lift - 1. - the force that results from air passing by a sail, or water past a keel, that moves the boat forward and sideways. 2. - a change in wind direction which lets the boat head up.

Line - a nautical rope.

Low side - the leeward side of the boat.

Lubber's line - a small post in a compass used to help determine a course or a bearing.

Luff - 1. - the forward edge of a sail.
2. - the fluttering of a sail caused by aiming too close to the wind.

Luff groove - the slot into which the luff of a sail is inserted.

Luff tape - an attachment to the luff of a sail consisting of a small, internal boltrope inserted into the luff groove on a roller furling system.

Lull - a decrease in wind speed for a short duration.

M

Magnetic - in reference to magnetic north rather than true north.

Mainmast - the taller of two masts on a boat.

Mainsail (MAIN-sil) - the sail hoisted on the mast of a sloop or cutter or the sail hoisted on the mainmast of a ketch or yawl.

Mainsheet - the controlling line for the mainsail.

Marlinspike - a pointed tool used to loosen knots.

Mast - the large aluminum or wooden pole in the middle of a boat from which the mainsail is set.

Masthead - the top of the mast.

Masthead fly - a wind direction indicator on top of the mast.

Mast step - the structure that the bottom of the mast sits on.

Mizzen - the small aftermost sail on a ketch or yawl hoisted on the mizzen mast.

Mooring - a permanently anchored ball or buoy to which a boat can be tied.

N

Nautical mile - a distance of 6076 feet, equaling one minute of the earth's latitude.

Navigation Rules - laws established to prevent collisions on the water.

No-Go Zone - an area into the wind in which a boat cannot produce power to sail.

Nun - a red, even-numbered, cone-shaped buoy marking the right side of a channel as you return to port. Nuns are usually paired with cans.

O

Offshore wind - wind blowing off (away from) the land.

Offshore - away from or out of sight of land.

Off the wind - sailing downwind.

On the wind - sailing upwind, close-hauled.

Outboard - 1. - outside the rail of a boat. 2. - a portable engine.

Outhaul - the controlling line attached to the clew of a mainsail used to tension the foot of the sail.

Overpowered - a boat that is heeling too far because it has too much sail up for the amount of wind.

Overtaking - a boat that is catching up to another boat and about to pass it.

P

Painter - the line attached to the bow of a dinghy.

Pay out - to ease a line.

Pinching - sailing too close to the wind.

Pintle - small metal extensions on a rudder that slides into a gudgeon on the transom. The gudgeon/pintle fitting allows the rudder to swing back and forth.

Point - to steer close to the wind.

Points of sail - boat directions in relation to wind direction, i.e., close-hauled, beam reaching, broad reaching, and running.

Port - 1. - the left side of a boat when facing forward. 2. - a harbor. 3. - a window in a cabin on a boat.

Port tack - sailing on any point of sail with the wind coming over the port side of the boat.

Prevailing wind - typical or consistent wind conditions.

Puff - an increase in wind speed for a short duration.

GLOSSARY

Pulpit - a stainless steel guardrail at the bow and stern of some boats.

Pushpit - a stainless steel guardrail at the stern of some boats.

Push-pull principle - the explanation of how sails generate power.

Q

Quarter - the sides of the boat near the stern.

Quick stop rescue - a maneuver used to return to a person or object in the water

R

Rail - the outer edges of the deck.

Rake - the angle of the mast.

Range - the alignment of two objects that indicate the middle of a channel.

Reach - one of several points of sail across the wind.

"Ready about" - the command given to the crew to prepare to tack.

"Ready to jibe" - the command given to the crew to prepare to jibe.

Reef - to reduce the size of a sail.

Reeve - to pass a line through a cringle or block.

Rhumb line - a straight course between two points.

Rig - 1. - the design of a boat's mast(s), standing rigging, and sail plan. 2. - to prepare a boat to go sailing.

Rigging - the wires and lines used to support and control sails.

Right-of-way - the right of the stand-on vessel to hold its course.

Roach - the sail area aft of a straight line running from the head to the clew of a sail.

Rode - line and chain attached from the boat to the anchor.

Roller furling - a mechanical system to roll up a headsail (jib) around the headstay.

Rudder - the underwater fin that is controlled by the tiller to deflect water and steer the boat.

Run - (point of sail) sailing with the wind coming directly behind the boat.

Running rigging - lines and hardware used to control the sails.

S

Sail cover - the protective cover used to preserve sails when they are not in use.

Sail ties - pieces of line or webbing used to tie the mainsail to the boom when reefing or storing the sail.

Schooner - a two-masted boat whose foremast is usually shorter than its mainmast.

Scope - the ratio of the amount of anchor rode deployed to the distance from the bow to the bottom.

Scull - to propel a boat by swinging the rudder back and forth.

Scupper - cockpit or deck drain.

Sea breeze - a wind that blows over the sea and onto the land.

Seacock - a valve which opens and closes a hole through the hull for saltwater needed on board or discharge.

Secure - make safe or cleat.

Set - 1. - the direction of a current. 2. - to trim the sails.

Shackle - a metal fitting at the end of a line used to attach the line to a sail or another fitting.

Shake out - to remove a reef and restore the full sail.

Sheave - the rotating wheel inside a block or fitting.

Sheet - 1. - (*noun*) the line which is used to control the sail by easing it out or trimming it in. 2. - (*verb*) to trim a sail.

Shoal - shallow water that may be dangerous.

Shroud - standing rigging at the side of the mast.

Singlehanded - sailing alone.

S-Jibe - the controlled method of jibing with the mainsail crossing the boat under control and the boat's path making an "S" shaped course.

Skeg - a vertical fin in front of the rudder.

Skipper - the person in charge of the boat.

Slip - a parking area for a boat between two docks in a marina.

Sloop - a single-masted sailboat with mainsail and headsail.

Snub - to hold a line under tension by wrapping it on a winch or cleat.

Sole - the floor in a cockpit or cabin.

Spar - a pole used to attach a sail on a boat, for example, the mast, the boom, a gaff.

Spinnaker - a large billowing headsail used when sailing downwind.

Splice - the joining of two lines together by interweaving their strands.

Spreader - a support strut extending athwartships from the mast used to support the mast and guide the shrouds from the top of the mast to the chainplates.

Spring line - a dockline running forward or aft from the boat to the dock to keep the boat from moving forward or aft.

Squall - a short intense storm with little warning.

Stability - a boat's ability to resist tipping (heeling).

Stanchions - stainless steel supports at the edge of the deck which hold the lifelines.

Standing rigging - the permanent rigging (usually wire) of a boat, including the forestay, backstay, and shrouds.

Stand-on vessel - the vessel or boat with the right-of-way.

Starboard - when looking from the stern toward the bow, the right side of the boat.

Starboard tack - sailing on any point of sail with the wind coming over the starboard side of the boat.

Stay - a wire support for a mast, part of the standing rigging.

Staysail (STAY-sil) - on a cutter, a second small "inner jib," attached between the bow and the mast.

Steer - to control the direction of a boat, using the tiller or wheel, in order to maintain the desired course.

Stem - the forward tip of the bow.

Step - the area in which the base of the mast fits.

Stern - the aft part of the boat.

Stow - to store properly.

Swamped - filled with water.

T

Tack - 1. - a course on which the wind comes over one side of the boat, i.e., port tack, starboard tack. 2. - to change direction by turning the bow through the wind. 3. - the lower forward corner of a sail.

Tackle - a sequence of blocks and line that provides a mechanical advantage.

Tail - to hold and pull a line from behind a winch.

Telltales - 1. - pieces of yarn or sailcloth material attached to sails which indicate when the sail is properly trimmed. 2. - wind direction indicators attached to standing rigging.

Tide - the rise and fall of water level due to the gravitational pull of the sun and moon.

Tiller - a long handle, extending into the cockpit, which directly controls the rudder.

Tiller extension - a handle attached to the tiller which allows the helmsman to sit further out to the side.

Toe rail - a short aluminum or wooden rail around the outer edges of the deck.

Topping lift - a line used to hold the boom up when the mainsail is lowered or stowed.

Topsides - the sides of the boat between the waterline and the deck.

Transom - the vertical surface of the stern.

Traveler - a track or bridle that controls sideways (athwartships) movement of the mainsail.

Trim - 1. - to pull in on a sheet. 2. - how a sail is set relative to the wind.

Trimaran - a three-hulled sailing vessel.

True wind - the actual speed and direction of the wind when standing still.

Tune - to adjust a boat's standing rigging.

Turnbuckle - a mechanical fitting attached to the lower ends of stays, allowing for the standing rigging to be adjusted.

U

Underway - to be under the power of sail or engine.

Unrig - to stow sails and rigging when the boat is not in use.

Upwind - toward the direction of the wind.

USCG - abbreviation for United States Coast Guard.

V

Vang - see **boom vang**.

Vessel - any sailboat, powerboat or ship.

W

Wake - waves caused by a boat moving through the water.

Waterline - the horizontal line on the hull of a boat where the water surface should be.

Weather helm - the boat's tendency to head up toward the wind, which occurs when a sailboat is overpowered.

Weather side - see **windward side**.

Whip - to bind together the strands at the end of a line.

Whisker pole - a pole, temporarily mounted between the mast and the clew of a jib, used to hold the jib out and keep it full when sailing downwind.

Winch - a deck-mounted drum with a handle offering mechanical advantage used to trim sheets. Winches may also be mounted on the mast to assist in raising sails.

Windward - toward the wind.

Windward side - the side of a boat or a sail closest to the wind.

Wing-and-wing - sailing downwind with the jib set on the opposite side of the mainsail.

Working sails - the mainsail and standard jib.

Working sheet - the leeward jib sheet that is being used to trim the jib.

Y

Yawl - a two-masted boat with its mizzen (after) mast shorter than its mainmast and located aft of the rudder post.

US Sailing Basic Keelboat Certification

The Basic Keelboat graduate will have successfully demonstrated the ability to responsibly skipper and crew a simple daysailing keelboat in familiar waters in light to moderate wind and sea conditions.

Recommended Equipment: It is recommended that Basic Keelboat Certification courses and examinations be conducted on 18' to 27' daysailing sloop-rigged keelboats with tiller steering and with adequate equipment inventory to complete all required certification outcomes.

Prerequisite: There is no prerequisite for Basic Keelboat Certification.

Certification Requirements: Basic Keelboat Certification requires the successful completion of the following knowledge and skill requirements. These requirements are expected to be able to be performed safely with confident command of the boat in familiar waters with a wind range of 5 to 15 knots. Some regions may have stronger prevailing conditions, which are acceptable if the candidate can safely control the boat and be aware of his or her limitations in these conditions. The certified candidate will be able to skipper a tiller-steered keelboat up to 27 feet in length.

Practical Skills

Preparation to Sail:
1. Demonstrate ability to recognize and forecast prevailing local weather conditions.
2. Demonstrate how to properly board a boat.
3. Perform a presail check for the boat's flotation integrity, safety and legally required equipment, and crew indoctrination.
4. Demonstrate the proper rigging of the sails, halyards, sheets, blocks, and winches.
5. Check all other equipment specific to your boat not indicated above.

Crew Operations and Skills:
6. Demonstrate how to put on a life jacket.
7. Demonstrate tying and use of knots: stopper knot, bowline, cleat hitch and square knot.
8. Demonstrate the use of these sail controls: halyards, sheets, Cunningham/downhaul and outhaul.

Leaving the Dock or Mooring:
9. Demonstrate appropriate helmsman and crew coordination and skills for departure suitable to the conditions: raising sails, line handling, casting off and boathandling.

Boat Control in Confined Waters:
10. Demonstrate in close quarters under sail: starting, stopping, speed control, tacking, jibing, steering control, sail luffing, the No-Go Zone, getting out of irons, backing the jib, and crew coordination and communication.
11. Demonstrate sailing a predetermined closed course and maneuvering around obstacles.

Navigation:
12. Point out Aids to Navigation in the harbor and local waters that you are sailing, and respond accordingly.

Navigation Rules, International-Inland:
13. Demonstrate use of Navigation Rules while sailing.

Boat Control in Open Water:
14. Demonstrate proper sail trim with accurate sheet adjustment of the main and headsails. Make use of the sail telltales and identify points of sail.
15. Perform a heaving-to maneuver.
16. When appropriate, demonstrate sailing "by the lee" and explain the inherent dangers involved.

Heavy Weather Sailing:
17. Demonstrate how to reef and/or depower sails.

Overboard Rescue Methods:
18. Properly demonstrate one of the overboard rescue methods, which is most appropriate for: your sailing ability, boat type, crew experience, wind and sea conditions, and maintaining constant visual contact with the PIW.

Safety and Emergency Procedures:
19. Explain the proper procedure for using an approved distress signal.

Returning to the Dock or Mooring:
20. Demonstrate appropriate helmsman and crew coordination and skills for arrival under sail and/or power suitable to the conditions: boathandling, deploying fenders, stopping, tying up and lowering sails. Explain at least two different approach plans for other conditions.

Securing the Boat Properly:
21. Demonstrate stowing of sails, rigging and equipment. Thoroughly clean the boat, and install any covers.
22. Check both the electrical and bilge systems for dock operation if required.
23. Check the locks on companionway, lockers and hatches. Make a final check of docklines, spring lines and fender placement.

Knowledge

Preparation to Sail:
1. Describe personal preparation such as clothing and sun protection.

Crew Operations and Skills:
2. Be familiar with the nomenclature for basic parts of the boat, sails, battens and rigging.
3. Describe the proper use of life jackets and throwable flotation devices.
4. Describe the use of sail controls.
5. Explain potential electrical hazards such as overhead electrical wires and lightning.

Sailing Theory:
6. Describe basic sailboat design, sail theory and boat dynamics.
7. Explain how to read the wind and determine all points of sail.
8. Understand what is meant by the term "sailing by the lee" and explain the inherent dangers involved.

Leaving the Dock or Mooring:
9. Understand the effects of wind, tide and currents in relation to the boat and surrounding area while preparing to get underway.
10. Describe the differences and alternatives for leaving under sail and/or power in upwind, crosswind and downwind situations.

Navigation:
11. Be familiar with basic chart reading specific to your local waters.
12. Describe Aids to Navigation: buoys, daymarks, regulatory markers, and other markers specific to your local waters.

Navigation Rules, International-Inland:
13. Describe the Navigation Rules, International-Inland, for Stand-On and Give-Way sailboats and powerboats for collision avoidance and understand your state and local boating regulations.

Heavy Weather Sailing:
14. Describe weather warning sources.

Overboard Rescue Methods:
15. Understand the Quick-Stop and Figure-8 overboard rescue methods to include: constant visual contact with the person in water, communication, rescue plan, sequence of maneuvers, boathandling, course sailed, pickup approach and coming alongside the PIW (or simulated object).
16. Describe methods of getting a PIW on deck.

Safety and Emergency Procedures:
17. Be familiar with treatment of overheating, hypothermia and seasickness.
18. Describe the use and regulations for flares.
19. Be familiar with at least six different distress and emergency signals per Navigation Rule 37.
20. Be familiar with the U.S. Coast Guard requirements for safety equipment.

Anchoring Techniques:
21. Be familiar with anchoring procedures for emergency situations such as loss of boat control, sudden storms, prevention from going aground or injured crew situations.

Returning to the Dock or Mooring:
22. Describe the differences and alternatives for arrival under sail and/or power in upwind, crosswind and downwind situations.

US Sailing and your sport.

Since 1897 the United States Sailing Association (US Sailing) has provided support for American sailors at all levels of sailing — in all kinds of sailboats. The primary objective of its Training Program is to provide a national standard of quality instruction for all people learning to sail. The US Sailing Keelboat Certification System includes a series of books such as Basic Keelboat, a program of student certifications and an extensive educational and training program for instructors. It is one of the most highly developed and effective national training systems for students and sailing instructors and is recognized nationally and internationally.

US Sailing is a non-profit organization and the official National Governing Body of Sailing as designated by the U. S. Congress in the Amateur Sports Act. It has a national training program for sailors in dinghies, windsurfers, multihulls and keelboats. It is also the official representative to the International Sailing Federation (ISAF).

The US Sailing Keelboat Certification System is designed to develop safe, responsible and confident sailors who meet specific performance and knowledge standards. (See US Sailing Basic Keelboat Certification on page 88 for the Basic Keelboat standards.) There are other benefits for you as well. You can start at the Basic Keelboat certification level and progress through Basic Cruising, Bareboat Cruising, Coastal Navigation, and even go on to Coastal Passage Making, Celestial Navigation and Offshore Passage Making.

With your US Sailing certifications and experience documented in the Official Logbook, you will have a passport to cruising and chartering boats locally or nationally.

Basic Keelboat is intended as a supplement to your sailing lessons, rather than as a substitute for them. It was created to help you accelerate your learning curve and clarify your understanding of the concepts and techniques of sailing.

What Makes Sailing Special?

The sport of sailing is open to people of all ages, incomes and abilities. Sailing offers virtually limitless choices of boats, each with its own unique characteristics, and the opportunity to explore an adjacent cove or an exotic tropical location.

Most sailors will acquire entry-level skills quite rapidly. Mastering those skills is an experience that will be rewarding, exciting and pleasurable for a lifetime.

As you continue to sail, you will find that sailing is more than simply being pushed and pulled by the wind. For most people, sailing is meeting new friends, enjoying nature's beauty and challenge, and sharing a unique fellowship with all boaters. A tremendous camaraderie exists among sailors, particularly on the water, which makes sailing and the people who do it -very special.

What can US Sailing do for you?

US Sailing is committed to helping you discover and enjoy the beauty, relaxation, challenge and friendships of sailing. As part of this commitment we offer:

The Keelboat Certification System
with its various levels of training and certification:

Basic Keelboat. To responsibly skipper and crew a simple daysailing keelboat in familiar waters in light to moderate wind and sea conditions.

Basic Cruising. To responsibly skipper and crew an auxiliary powered cruising sailboat during daylight hours within sight of land in moderate wind and sea conditions.

Bareboat Cruising. To responsibly skipper, crew or bareboat charter an inboard auxiliary powered cruising sailboat within sight of land to a port or an anchorage during daylight hours in moderate to strong wind and sea conditions.

Coastal Navigation. To properly use traditional navigation techniques and electronic navigation for near coastal passage making.

Coastal Passage Making. To responsibly skipper and crew an inboard auxiliary powered cruising sailboat for coastal or offshore passages in strong to heavy conditions, including zero visibility and nighttime, in unfamiliar waters out of sight of land.

Celestial Navigation. To navigate using celestial techniques and integrating celestial with traditional navigation techniques.

Offshore Passage Making. To responsibly skipper and crew an inboard auxiliary powered cruising sailboat to any destination worldwide.

The Basic Windsurfing Certification which is available for entry level sailors.

The Small Boat Certification System which is available for dinghy, daysailer and multihull sailors in two wind speed ranges: light and heavy air.

Plus many other useful services:
US Sailing certified instructors help you achieve new skills and knowledge using up to date and safe methods.

Course materials, including this book, presented in a highly visual format to help you gain competency and confidence in your sailing skills and knowledge.

The Official Logbook, recognized nationally and internationally, to document your US Sailing certifications and experience when chartering boats nationally.

A website of accredited US Sailing schools, that use US Sailing certified instructors and US Sailing course materials. www.sailingcertification.com

US Sailing Safety-at-Sea seminars.

Racing Rules and handicap rating systems.

US Sailing membership makes you a part of the National Governing Body for the Sport of Sailing as well as giving you discounts on products and services that US Sailing offers. www.ussailing.org

Nautonics
↳ depths

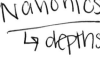

Day 1

Notes

LOA: length overall- Bow to stern

LWL: Load waterline length - bow & stern exiting water

Draft: Boat depth in water

Freebord: edge of deck to waterline

Abeam : 90° from beam

• Primary Purpose of standing rigging → keep mast upright
   ↳ [mast, boom, jibstay/forestay, backstay, shrouds, spreaders]

• Sheets: move sails in & out

• Halyards: move sails up & down

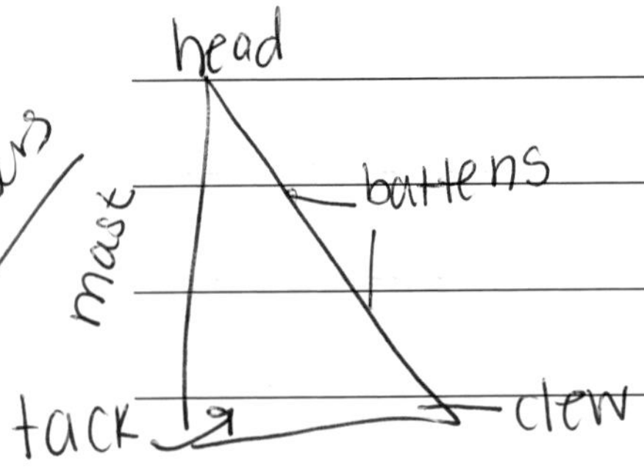

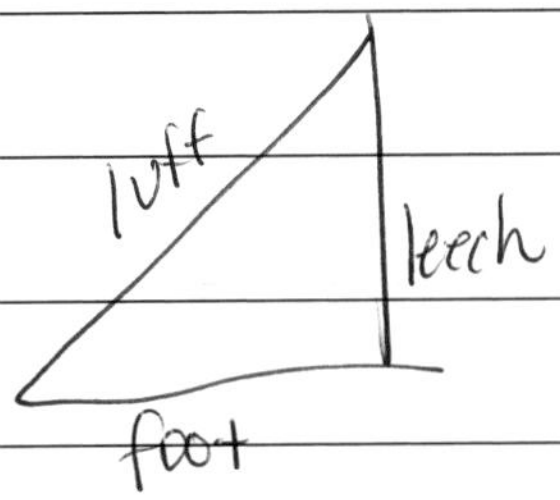

head

Corners

mast

battens

tack → clew

luff

leech

foot

main

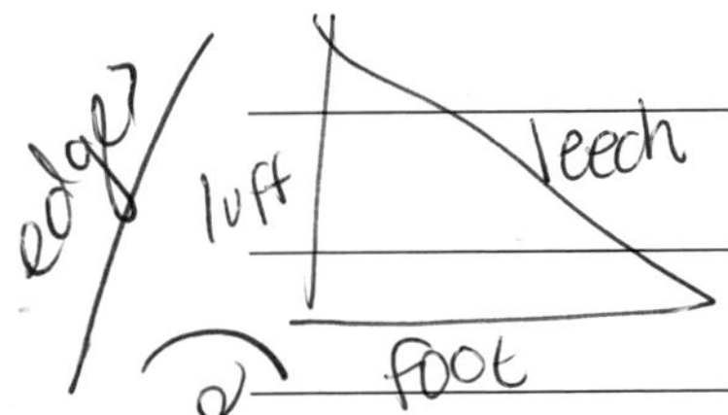

edge

luff

leech

foot

Jibing: when stern goes through wind (no-go-zone)

"Tack" | multiple meanings

• Tack: forward lower corner of sail

• Tack: Boat's heading in relation to wind
   ↳ opposite side of where boom is, is ___ tack

• Tacking: change direction from one side of wind to the other (bow goes through wind → nogo zone)

S P PORT tack

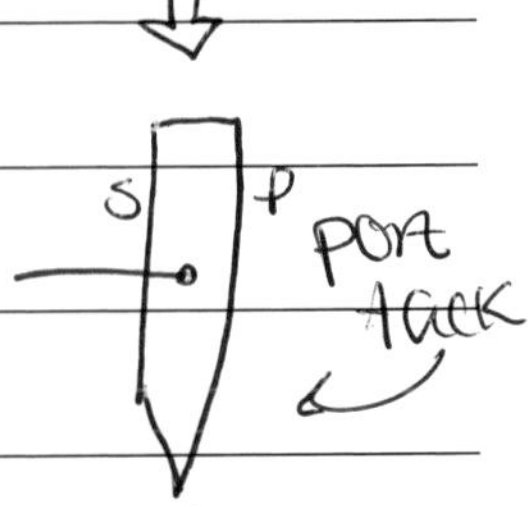

| Day 1 |

No-go-zone
⇩ /90°\ anything in this 90°
is "no go" and too much
into the wind
↳ in "irons"

Notes

Set of sail: When raised sail is full of wind

Luffing: Flapping along luff of sail →◢
↳① Poorly trimmed ② too much into the wind

• Wind is dead ahead (sails will luff, sails stream aft, boat stops) ↳ all of the above

• Rudder steers the boat, tiller turns the rudder

• Shooting: Head into the wind, glide to a stop

Get out of irons: starboard tack
1) Back jib to port ↗ 2) Bow swings to starboard 3) trim sails for wind direction

| Points of Sailing |

1) closehauled: Sailing close to wind as possible → put sails in tight

2) Reaching: wind across boat   3) Running: wind behind boat
↳ ease sails out a bit   port tack   ↳ sails all the way out 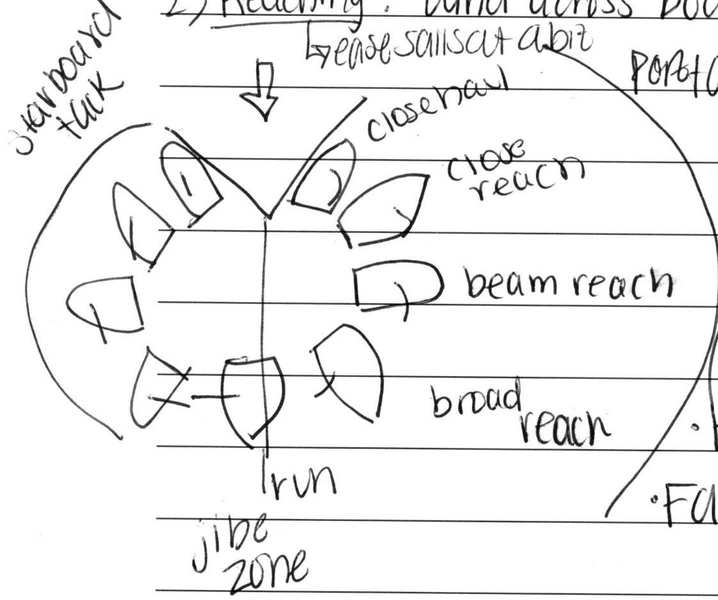
⇩ closehaul
close reach
beam reach   • Beat: tacking back & forth
Starboard tack   "Heading up" = trim sails
broad reach   changing course w/o jib and/or tacking:
run   • Hardening up - turn boat towards wind
jibe zone   • Falling off - Turn boat away from wind

Stop knot: 1, 2, pull it through. ⟨⟨⟨⟨⟨⟨⟨⟨
Bowline: Rabbit goes in hole, around the tree, back in hole

squincl meat: someone who sits on othervside to

The wind: ondock

luff /\ leech
(chord)

Day 2

Prevent sideslippage

wind ↓
leward / windward

backstay
outhaul
sheet tension
cunningham
halyard
boom vang / traveler

Notes

Leeward: Away from the wind   Windward: Towards the wind

• Steer away from angry telltale (tiller boat same side, wheel is opposite)
  ↳ only on close haul, when sails are tight
• trim sail more towards angry telltale if not on a close haul
• "Off the wind" sailing downwind (push mode only) → jib sometimes can't catch wind
• Full sails: deep draft (deep curve)   • Flat sails: shallow draft, less powerful, high winds (use in high winds)
• cunningham: tightens luff   ↳ outhaul tension, backstay tension, cunningham tension, halyard tension, mainsheet ease, traveler ease, boom vang tension

• True wind: changes strengths (puffs & lulls), changes direction
  ↳ veering: clockwise   backs: counterclockwise   heads: wind towards bow *
     lifts: wind towards stern

• Apparent wind: true + boat speed

• Sailing by the lee: wind is on same side as boom

man overboard

tack, don't jibe

release jibe

open
Transome: Back area of boat
• PICK UP a mooring: beam reach and shoot into the wind

X
↖

Day 3

Notes

- Center of Effort: combined effort of all sails when they're set
- Weather Healm: tendency for boat to turn towards wind (CE behind weather helm)
- Stand-on vessel: has right of way. maintain course & speed
- Giveway: Alter course to avoid collision 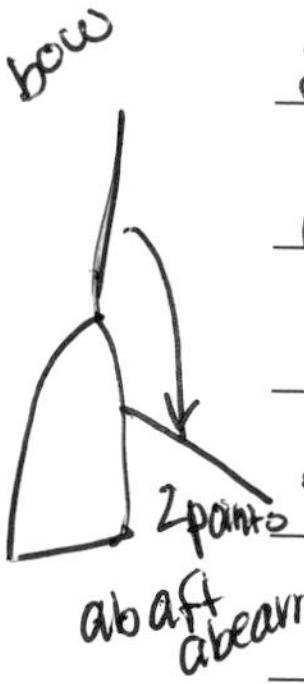
- same tack rule: • Leeward boat ~~has right of way~~ right of way
- Opposite tack rule: Starboard stands on
- Overtaking rule: boat ahead has right of way 
- When engine is on, powerboat → any boat in danger zone has right of way, right has right of way
- red on port, green on starboard, white on stern
  - ↳ sailing under power add white on mast 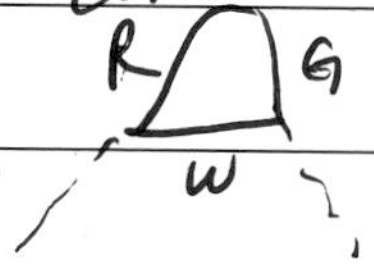
- maintain control underway: reduce sail (reef mainsail, change jib)
- extreme conditions: douse all sails, anchor, broadcast position channel 16
- Ratio of anchor line is 7:1

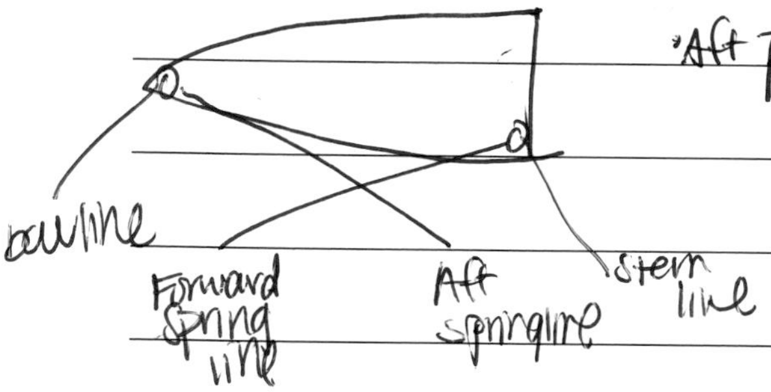

bow

2 points

ab aft abeam

R W G

• Aft protects forward, forward protects behind

bow line

Forward Spring line

Aft spring line

stern line

- Going out   green   Coming back in   green
- red   red

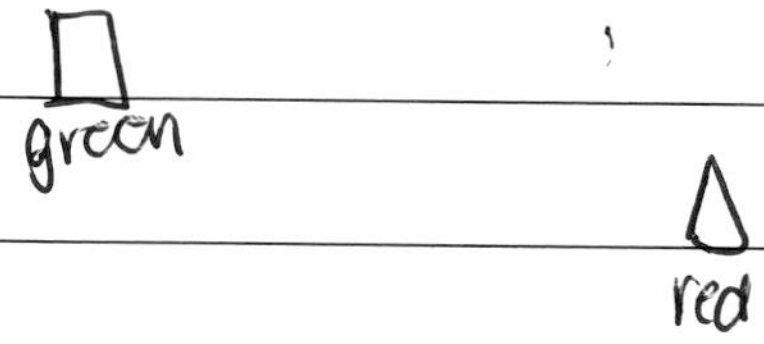

Red. Right. Return

R